## PRAISE FOR KYLE W

"Kyle Willkom is a true advocate for our young people. I've seen firsthand how his authentic storytelling, infectious humor, and thoughtful lessons inspire young people to lean into their leadership. He has spoken to thousands of our students and educators and knocked it out of the park every time. This book is yet one more reason why Kyle connects with students where most fail. The valuable insight Kyle Willkom delivers in this book provides actionable steps for students to change their mindset and become the leaders they were meant to be. This book is a must for not only students, but also, any person that works with young people. This book is a must read for anyone interested in moving their leadership from average to exceptional."

—Michelle McGrath, *Ed. D, Executive Director*
*Wisconsin Association of Student Councils*

"We feel very fortunate to have hosted Kyle at our school. He was everything we were looking for in a speaker/workshop facilitator: professional, engaging, honest, and practical. Most importantly, he effortlessly connected to our students and the challenges facing today's teenagers. Our student leaders left their workshops armed with many tools and resources to move and take action to attain their future goals for themselves-- and for the entire school. Our student body respected Kyle's unique humor, personal stories, and impressive accomplishments. He made all of our students reflect, laugh, and feel confident that life's challenges can be met head on by empowering them to take action starting that day. I highly recommend Kyle for any of your workshop, training, or assembly needs!"

—Bill Martin, *Director of Student Activities,*
  *Co-Director of Oratory Prep Summer Academy*
  *Oratory Prep School, Summit, New Jersey*

"As a Marketing and Business Education Teacher and DECA Advisor, I have been partnering with Kyle for many years. I have utilized Kyle's online resources, referenced his books, and have had him as a guest speaker in my classroom many times. Whether it be through his books, his online materials, or speaking to groups, Kyle connects with all his audiences. Kyle relies on his own life experiences to provide examples that are especially meaningful to teachers, students, and anyone striving for personal and/or professional growth. This book is no different! Not only does Kyle talk about the characteristics needed for leadership, but he provides practical methods and steps to get readers to actively think like a leader! No matter who you are or what role you play in society, you will walk away with a better understanding of what it means to think and act like a leader to help you improve all aspects of your life after reading this book."

—Ashley Tessmer, *High School Marketing and Business Education Teacher*
Wisconsin Rapids Lincoln High School

"Dynamic. Entertaining. Inspiring. Impactful. Relatable. Engaging. These words are the first to come to mind when I reflect on Kyle's multiple interactions and trainings with our Tennessee CTSO members."

—Steven Mitchell, *State Advisor*
Tennessee DECA and FBLA

"Kyle captivated the audience at the Kentucky 4-H Teen Conference, his energy was exactly what our teens needed to start an amazing week at our high school leadership conference."

—Rachel Noble, *Extension Specialist*
Kentucky 4-H

"Kyle's speaking style is the right mix of humor, storytelling, kindness, and inspiration. He has a magical gift for connecting with his audience, both kids and adults. We have had good speakers come to our conventions over the years, but we have never had the amount of positive feedback like we received after Kyle spoke for us."

—David Bowe, *Director*
Texas Association of Student Councils, District 18

## ALSO BY KYLE WILLKOM

Wake Up Call
The Thinking Dilemma

Empowering High School Students to
Think Positive, Take Action, and Create Change

# ACTION PACKED LEADERSHIP

## KYLE WILLKOM

Copyright © 2020 by Kyle Willkom

All rights reserved. No part of this publication may be reproduced, stored in a retrieval system, or transmitted by any means – electronic, mechanical, photographic (photocopying), recording, or otherwise – without prior permission in writing from the author.

Printed in the United States of America

ISBN: 9798664375770

Cover design by Mila Milic and interior formatting by James Saleska.

For more information, visit www.kylewillkom.com.

## AUTHOR'S NOTE

While this book is about *action*, you'll notice much of it focuses on positive and intentional *thought*. This is not a mistake. *Action Packed Leadership* is about building the *mindset* of a leader – and in doing so, empowering each individual who picks up this book to take action in his or her own unique way every day.

With the proper mindset, young leaders can do anything.

# CONTENTS

Introduction .................................................................... 11

**CHAPTER 1 PREFACE:** Pasta Dinners ................................. 19

**CHAPTER 1:** Leadership Communication ........................ 23

**CHAPTER 2 PREFACE:** The DECA Guy ............................. 53

**CHAPTER 2:** Personal Branding ....................................... 57

**CHAPTER 3 PREFACE:** More Than a Game ...................... 73

**CHAPTER 3:** Taking Initiative .......................................... 77

**CHAPTER 4 PREFACE:** Florida or Bust ............................. 91

**CHAPTER 4:** Project Management .................................... 95

**CHAPTER 5 PREFACE:** I Just Want a Cheeseburger ......... 109

**CHAPTER 5:** Networking ................................................ 115

**CHAPTER 6 PREFACE:** No Hice La Tarea ....................... 131

**CHAPTER 6:** Time Management .................................... 135

**CHAPTER 7 PREFACE:** There's Got to Be a Better Way .................. 149

**CHAPTER 7:** Working Smarter ......................................................... 153

**CHAPTER 8 PREFACE:** Murphy's Law .............................................. 163

**CHAPTER 8:** Public Speaking ............................................................ 167

**CHAPTER 9 PREFACE:** Starting Somewhere .................................... 175

**CHAPTER 9:** Building Trust .............................................................. 179

**CHAPTER 10 PREFACE:** Life is a Marathon ..................................... 189

**CHAPTER 10:** Staying Motivated ...................................................... 193

**CHAPTER 11 PREFACE:** You're Fired ............................................... 201

**CHAPTER 11:** Maintaining Relationships ......................................... 205

**CHAPTER 12 PREFACE:** You Can't Stay Forever .............................. 213

**CHAPTER 12:** Building a Legacy ....................................................... 215

Eddie Would Go ................................................................................. 221

Acknowledgments .............................................................................. 225

About the Author ............................................................................... 227

Interviews ........................................................................................... 229

Notes .................................................................................................. 230

# INTRODUCTION

**Let's start with an obvious statement:**

*Student leaders think.*

This statement is not exactly mind-blowing. They study, organize, and plan thoughtfully and deliberately.

**One more obvious statement:**

*All students think.*

It's not exactly rocket science. We're human beings, right? We all have thoughts going through our heads at all times.

So why am I telling you the obvious?

If student leaders think and all students think, student leaders must be *thinking differently*.

They must be approaching the world with an alternate perspective, and using this perspective to get ahead in school and in life.

The key to the student leader is not simply *that* thinking is taking place, but *how* thinking is taking place.

I've realized through extensive work with high school students across the United States as well as countless conversations with speakers, educators, professors, and leadership experts – **a simple change in mentality can make all the difference between an average student and an exceptional student.**

A change of mindset can lead any young person to more beneficial relationships, higher involvement in activities inside and outside of school, and – would you believe it – better grades.

One simple switch – just one – in the way students perceive themselves and the world around them can affect everything. A simple change in mindset can put young people in a better position to get internships and jobs later in life, make and save more money, or even find their soulmate.

Incorporating a new, more effective mindset into day-to-day life can lead any student down a new, surprising, and overwhelmingly positive path.

*Thinking differently* can change everything.

. . .

What if I told you this leadership mentality can be learned?

What if I told you the thoughts of student leaders have been documented, and you have unlimited access to them? These student leaders not only wanted to share what they *did*, but how they *thought* about what they did.

What if, today, I could share with you all the secrets to becoming a leader before you've even finished high school?

You're in luck.

I'm not writing this book simply to write another book – writing two books was hard enough! I'm writing this book for you – to bring you value and to share the secrets of student leadership.

It is my hope this book becomes your guiding force in leadership.

I hope it proves to be the most valuable book you have read up until this point in your life. I believe this book can make an enormous impact on the students who are fortunate enough to pick it up and dedicated enough to put the words on these pages into practice. When using the framework outlined in the pages to come, young people will be poised to feel more comfortable in their own skin, build more meaningful relationships, get better grades, make more money, and excel in just about any leadership role they take on or are thrust into.

I believe this book can be just as meaningful for those who work with young people on a regular basis – the teachers, coaches, advisors, and principals who are constantly looking for better ways to connect with the students they serve.

I will do my best to provide real, practical ways for you to become a better leader in your school, community, and later in your life.

Because the truth is:

**Any student is capable of being a leader.**[1]

There are specific actions, which later turn to habits, young leaders employ which make them more successful than other students, and these habits are not secrets (or at least they won't be after reading further). When the lessons here are incorporated into daily life, any student can be exceptional.

Of course, simply thinking differently is not enough.

After reading that statement, you might be saying to yourself, "Thinking differently is not enough? Then why did you just tell me all about how student leaders think differently?"

It's a fair point –think for a moment about a time in your life you got into trouble for something. It may have been when you were little or it may have been fairly recent. What happened? Did you get yelled at? Did you get detention? What did you do to deserve these punishments?

---

[1] Yes, I really believe this.

You'll notice I didn't say, "What did you *think* to deserve these punishments.

I'm guessing whatever it is that got you into trouble was not because you *thought* something; if I were a betting person, I would put money on it being something you *said* or *did* that got you into trouble.

Thoughts alone won't get you into trouble; behavior will.

In this same way, thoughts alone will not make you an exceptional leader; your actions will.

So why do I focus so much on thoughts within this book?

Thoughts direct actions and actions direct outcomes – a change in the way you *think* will change the way you *act*. This is the key to *Action Packed Leadership*.

The more you *think* about the right things, the more your *actions* will reflect them. When your thoughts and actions become consistent, they are then called habits.

Naturally, as seen in the figure below, analyzing the outcomes you get from your actions will lead you to new thoughts, which will lead to new actions, which will lead to new outcomes.

It is your job to consistently check in with your thoughts to ensure you will regularly take effective action.

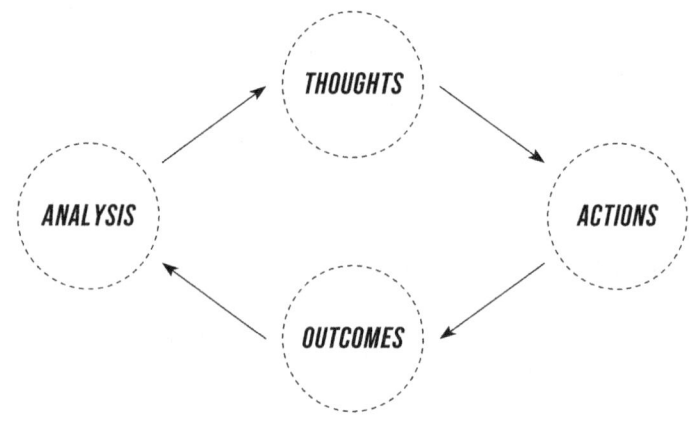

This book is intended to help you develop a higher level of thought.

This higher level of thought can then be used to become more successful as a communicator, innovator, and leader. The higher level of brain power we'll discuss throughout this book will give you the ability to take your life in new directions, based in positive thought. If you already love the direction your life is headed, stay with me. You may just find what you need to reach your true potential, whatever path you may be on.

> **QUOTABLE:**
>
> *"What seizes your imagination will affect everything."*
>
> —PEDRO ARRUPE

Before we dive in – I'd like to make sure we're on the same page.[2]

I've heard the term "Leadership" defined lots of different ways.

For the purpose of this book, I'd like us to have a definition we can all agree upon. So this is it:

*A leader is someone whom others follow.*

Pretty simple, right? With this definition, there are a lot of different kinds of young leaders out there – from the captain of a sports team to the president of a student organization to simply the leader of a group of friends.

I didn't write this only for the best and brightest students at school.

This book is just as much for the young people wondering, "Am I a leader?" as it is for the standout students already in leadership positions. It is for every style of leader – from the introverted, subtle leader to the bold, aggressive leader.

If I had to guess, I'd bet you could think of one person you may be leading right now – intentionally or unintentionally. Believe it or not, you are already a leader. This book is for you.

Action Packed Leadership is also for the adults who are passionately working to develop young leaders. Learning the mindset of a leader is

---

[2] Figuratively, of course – because you're obviously on page 15.

a life-long pursuit and doesn't end when you're no longer considered a "student."

Personally, I believe anyone could read this book and find value in these pages. While I wrote it to apply to students (from middle school to high school) – I'm certain it will be equally as valuable to adults (from middle-aged to high-stressed; only kidding).

So whether you're a struggling Freshman, budding upperclassmen, class president, aspiring college attendee, teacher, advisor, coach, or parent, you are in the right place.

I'll take you through an inside-out approach to leadership. It differs from other leadership books in that the primary message is not about *doing the right things,* but rather *being the right person.*

The framework for leadership you will read about assumes there are several "Action Categories" directly associated with our *thoughts* and *feelings.* This framework of leadership picks apart the underlying drivers of these "Action Categories." Based on both research and experience, below are the "Action Categories" in which *thinking differently* can make a world of difference – these will be our primary focus.

- Leadership Communication
- Personal Branding
- Taking Initiative
- Project Management
- Networking
- Time Management
- Working Smart
- Public Speaking
- Building Trust
- Maintaining Relationships
- Building a Legacy

When Former FBLA President Niel Patel was asked how he became the leader of a national organization while in high school, his first answer was telling: "One of the things I did was talk to people who had already done it. This gave me a head start through shared knowledge."

In the same spirit, you'll find stories and quotes from standout student leaders throughout the pages to come – hopefully everyone reading will learn from their shared knowledge.

I've organized the topics above so each chapter can be read and implemented on their own – feel free to read the topics of interest to you out of order. However, the topics become most effective when utilized together. Each lesson overlaps with the ones before it and the ones yet to come to build an entire framework for *thoughtful leadership* that naturally flows into *action*.

Within these pages, you'll find insights and anecdotes from student leaders as well as quotes, fun facts, and helpful hints to make the road to leadership a little easier.

As you read, apply the concepts to your own life and complete the *Action Packed Discussion Questions* at the end of each chapter.

When you consistently *apply* what you learn in this book to your life, each section will bring you closer to being a dynamic student leader.

Are you ready?

**It's time to Think Positive, Take Action, and Create Change.**

*Kyle Willkom*

Kyle Willkom

Chapter 1 Preface

# PASTA DINNERS

Early in my high school career, I learned the value of effective communication in a not-so-pretty way.

I love sports.

I have always loved sports.

I grew up with three older siblings who all became college athletes. I was always watching college basketball or cheering on the Packers on Sundays.[3]

When I was a sophomore in high school, I became one of two underclassmen to make the varsity soccer team and the only underclassmen to make the varsity basketball team.

It was an honor to be selected to play at the highest level of high school athletics in not one, but two sports as just a sophomore.

Each team presented different ups and downs, but from a communication standpoint, my experiences could not have been more different.

---

[3] At first I didn't believe it, but Bears fans can be student leaders too.

After the varsity soccer team was posted, the first phone call I received was from the goalie on the team – a senior named Ben. He told me he was excited that I was going to be a part of the team and knowing that I didn't have my driver's license yet, asked if I needed rides to practice. I was happy to accept.

He drove me and another underclassmen soccer player named Ethan to practice every day after school.[4]

The upperclassmen players on the team began following Ben's lead and inviting the underclassmen to pasta dinners before games and to play cards on weekends.

The team dynamic went further than the soccer field and the success we started to see reflected our chemistry.

Our soccer team went on to win the conference championship for the first time in school history, and I, one of the youngest players on the team, scored the game-winning goal in the conference championship game.[5]

Here's where things change.

My varsity basketball team could not have been further from this experience. No phone call to welcome me onto the team. No pasta dinners. No playing cards on weekends.

On the first day of practice, I showed up to find a small group of seniors sitting in a circle getting their shoes on, a small group of juniors in a separate circle, and me. I was the only sophomore on the team, and I didn't know much about the older players.

---

[4] Although, none of us did much talking on these drives because Ben loved his music LOUD.

[5] The other sophomore on the team that year, Ethan, went on to play Division One soccer at Creighton University, and got drafted 10th overall in the MLS draft – he became an MLS All-Star and a member of the United States Men's National Team. He is still one of my best friends and wrote the foreword for my second book, The Thinking Dilemma.

Throughout the season, it became crystal clear the older players didn't want me on the team.

They thought I was taking playing time from the older guys, and they weren't happy about it. Because of this, they rarely talked to me and when they did, it was to yell at me for a play that didn't turn out right on the court.

The upperclassmen took it upon themselves to haze the "new guy," and made my season extremely difficult. On one occasion, a player spit on my food on the bus after a game, and I wasn't able to eat that evening during the 3-hour ride home.

To make matters worse, members of the coaching staff would hear about these things taking place and say things like, "You gotta learn to take a joke."

It may go without saying - our team had issues.

Some older players on the team tried to have my back at times, but after getting ridiculed for taking my side, they quickly stopped standing up for me.

We did not communicate well and it showed. It showed in how we treated each other at practice, it showed with how we talked to each other during games, and most importantly, it showed in the box score; we were one of the worst teams in the conference.

I wish I could tell you an awesome turn-around story about how we came back and had an amazing season – how we overcame our issues, banded together and won the conference title – but that story doesn't exist.

I'd be lying to you if I said my sophomore basketball season wasn't one of the worst experiences on a team I've ever had.

We played poorly. We lost a lot of games. We didn't have much fun, and we didn't like each other much either.

Were there things I could have done to make the experience better? Of course. Looking back, I would have done a lot of things differently, but those things don't always click when you're 16 years old.

There are obviously other factors playing roles in being successful in sports (and in life), but I've seen both effective and ineffective communication first-hand, and I know the difference each can make in the outcomes we see at the end of the day.

I've also witnessed countless examples of the positive and negative effects of communication in the lives of students I work with.

I've heard stories from both students and teachers in which a classic misunderstanding is the primary dramatic focal point of an issue.

Communication is hard.

Communicating with another human being takes energy and emotion from both sides.

In this chapter you'll see exactly how student leaders communicate. We'll discuss the energy and emotion it takes to communicate well, and I'll dive into what it looks like to create a winning communication style.

And if you haven't already in one way or another, you'll very quickly see the difference effective communication can make in your life.

Chapter 1

# LEADERSHIP COMMUNICATION

*"Tis better to be silent and be thought a fool, than to speak and remove all doubt."*

—Abraham Lincoln

As prospective student leaders, the skills you are developing now will aid you in high school, college, the work force, and beyond – and no skill is as essential in today's connected society as *leadership communication*.

Whether you want to be an artist, an accountant, or anything in between – clearly communicating your ideas is an indispensable skill that allows you to make connections, get involved, and lead others effectively.

Communication stems across verbal, non-verbal, text, e-mail, and social media platforms.

In this chapter, I'll explore how you can use each of these platforms to accomplish your goals as a leader.

More than anything – the key is to start now.

If you want to be effective in the working world someday, you should begin communicating effectively now – you can do so when you meet for a group project, organize an event, or interact with your parents, coaches, advisors, employers, teachers, and friends. The sooner you start, the easier it will be to communicate well over time.

Young leaders understand that with practice, communication will come more naturally.

When you've enhanced your ability to communicate, you will be in a better position to succeed.

So where does your communication journey begin on your path to student leadership?

I'm glad you asked.

## WHERE COMMUNICATION BEGINS

*"You want to know how to paint a perfect painting? It's easy. Make yourself perfect and then just paint naturally... the making of a painting isn't separate from the rest of your existence."*

—Robert M. Pirsig

Many times, communication is only as effective as the communicator.

It is not simply about *saying* the right things, but *being* the person who says the right things.

I've always believed in the sentiment that it is from the feelings of the *heart* that the mouth *speaks*.

This is the reason this entire book is about *thoughts*.

Think back to my high school soccer team – Ben communicated so well to us underclassmen because he first recognized that helping us grow and develop would only benefit our team in the future.

His desire for *greater team success* led him to make that first phone call.

He wasn't just communicating well because he thought it was the appropriate thing to do. He was communicating well to help our team reach a desired *outcome*.

Had my basketball team been "effective" at saying how they felt, they would probably have just called me names in a much more elegant way.[6]

The difference was not simply an *ability* to communicate, but the *sentiment* behind the communication.

It is not simply about *what* we say or even *how* we say it – the best communication is about *where* our communication stems from.

The best communication stems from *positive values*.

When we make a *firm decision* to ground our values in words such as compassion, kindness, generosity, service, and love,[7] these words become the foundation of our *character*.

Young people with great character communicate more effectively than others who have not yet made the firm decision to live by desirable values.

If you haven't yet made this decision, fear not!

The good news is you can make a decision to re-define your values every day. You can begin building a new foundation for your character right now, in this moment, as you're reading this book.

I mentioned you need to make a *firm decision*. I truly believe this.

Let's say today, you went up to someone you consider a leader and asked her if she wants a cigarette. Most likely, she would look at you strangely and say the words I'm sure you've heard before:

**"I'm not a smoker."**

---

[6] Which is still not helpful.

[7] And any other desirable quality for that matter – these are just a few examples.

This may seem insignificant, but I believe it has an important meaning.

Because she had already made the *firm decision* to not smoke cigarettes, her decision has become a part of her identity.

She didn't say, "I'm not smoking cigarettes right now," or "Not this time." By saying, "I'm not a *smoker*," she is figuratively saying, "What you're asking me *to do* is not *who I am*."

This is a big deal.

This is exactly what making a *firm decision* looks like – the foundation of our character literally changes our *identity*.

Crazy, right?

When we have grounded ourselves in positive values and built our character in a way that re-defines our entire *identity*, how could our communication skills not change for the better?

When a student leader's identity becomes filled with positive qualities such as kindness, compassion, generosity, and love, and he pushes his *thinking* daily to align with these qualities, his *communication* will naturally follow.

**In this way, the best student leaders challenge themselves to look inside before converting their thoughts into words.**

Average (or below average) students convert thoughts into words before evaluating their motivations – this tends to lead to communication driven by selfishness, drama, fear, hate, indifference, or other undesirable qualities.

The *thought* behind the words helps construct the proper words.

Are you starting to see how thinking like a leader can change everything? We just skimmed the surface on terms like *identity* and *character*, and yet it isn't rocket science to understand that the *firm decisions* we make based in *positive and intentional thought* will change us at the very core of our being. And when the core of who we are as people changes dramatically, it is no surprise that our words, texts, e-mails, even nonverbals will shift dramatically as well.

Before embarking on your journey to lead others, a few good questions to ask yourself might be:

- What adjectives would I use to define myself in the most ideal way?
- What firm decisions have I made in my life?
- Are my pursuits noble?[8]
- Will my efforts as a leader deliver positive outcomes for everyone involved (not just me)?
- Are my words coming from a place of kindness, patience, compassion, generosity, love, etc.?

When you feel your thoughts are ready to become words, the next sections will help you become more specific – we will dive deeper into how to communicate as a leader.

## FILLING YOUR CUP

You have good ideas – get them out there!

Developing the *thought* behind your words based in positive *values* and strong *character* is the basis for every communication lesson to come.

People often use the phrase the "tip of the iceberg." In this scenario, it is the opposite. *Character* is the base of your iceberg – it is the 90% that is so often unnoticed, but so vitally important to becoming an exceptional young leader.

Picture this – in your hand you have a cup and it is filled to the top. You look into the cup and get excited because you notice it is filled with your favorite drink. You bring the cup toward your lips and take a big swig expecting the deliciousness of your favorite drink to hit you like a refreshing wave of goodness. To your surprise, it does not taste like your favorite drink at all.

---

[8] I know, I know – no one says "noble" anymore, but there's a certain ring to "noble pursuits."

You immediately taste something so awful it causes you to spray the contents in your mouth across the rest of the room. Your friends laugh as you continue to try to get the taste out of your mouth. You look down at the cup that, just two seconds ago, held your favorite drink, except now you're staring at a dark brown, gooey substance that could only be wet mud…or worse – turns out this substance had been in the cup the whole time, it was simply hidden underneath your favorite drink. You couldn't see this substance initially because your favorite drink had been poured over top of it.

This is what happens when young people learn to *say* the right things before working to *be* the right person.

To be clear, I'm talking about **filling your cup from the bottom.**

If whoever handed you the deceptive cup you just drank from had started filling it with your favorite drink from the base, you would have had no issues. You would have enjoyed your favorite beverage and went on with your day.

However, the person who gave you this cup clearly didn't care about all the contents, just the contents on the surface that would make it appealing to drink.

When you fill your cup from the bottom, you don't have to worry about what's on the surface because it will simply be a reflection of what you filled it with.[9]

Communicating well is no different.

Student leaders define their values then speak from the heart. They don't simply tell other people what they want to hear, and they don't break from their character.

Student leaders fill their cup from the bottom, and let their character overflow.

This is a constant practice and most likely will take a lifetime to comprehend. Some important questions to ask yourself may be:

---

[9] You might want to read this sentence twice. It's important.

- What is currently in my cup?

    *Anger? Fear? Anxiety? Indifference? Jealousy?*
- If I could empty my cup right now, what would I begin to fill it with from the bottom?

    *Patience? Gratitude? Acceptance? Kindness? Generosity?*
- How do I start to *be* the right person instead of just learning to *say* the right things?

## KEYS TO COMMUNICATING AS A LEADER

Once you have worked on your values, identity, and character, there is still the 10% of the iceberg left on the surface. I'm talking about the *ability* to speak well, and the *confidence* to put your thoughts into the world through your *voice*.

Whether you are the captain of a sports team or simply want to give your opinion in class, speaking well will help you get your messages across in a way that connects.

Allow these tips to guide you:

### Listen

You'll notice that the first step to speaking well has nothing to do with speaking.

Everyone, not just young people, need to re-learn how to listen. We hear just fine – but are we actually listening?

Real listening takes patience. We've all been the person who is thinking about what we're going to say next while someone else is talking.

Listening well means taking in the full thought of the speaker without judgment or personal bias. It means hearing 100% of what she has to say before making assumptions or giving feedback. It means listening to understand as opposed to listening only to respond.

What you'll find when you begin to listen in this way is that you'll actually have *more* to say, not less.

Conversations will be more interesting. You already know everything *you* have to say, but something someone else says might surprise you, educate you, or challenge you.

**QUOTABLE:**

*"The biggest communication problem is we do not listen to understand. We listen to reply."*

—ANONYMOUS

Listening with interest helps you learn new things, and these new things will help you speak more intelligently when it is your turn.

Below is a short list of four ways you can listen better right now – but remember, it's not just about *doing it*, it's about *thinking about it* the right ways.

When we think about listening in the right way, we see it as valuable for our learning, growth, personal relationships, and know it will ultimately make us better communicators – the *thinking* behind your listening will help you make it more authentic, and you will *automatically* start to do it more in your life.

Keep an open mind when listening to others.

1. Let others complete their thoughts without interruption.
2. Focus your attention on what they are saying and not on what you will say next.
3. To show your interest, ask questions and stay engaged.
4. Listening well is getting harder and harder in our quick-response society. Everyone has a response for everything at all times.

You can be better.

Student leaders actively give attention to those they lead, and empower them to speak up both in one-on-one and group settings.

It's important to remember, student leaders aren't doing this out of charity – they don't do it because they think they *should*. They do it with a kind heart because they truly *want* to be a good listener, and they understand the value of giving someone their full attention.

## Be Clear

Next comes clarity.

People appreciate honesty and directness. Skirting around what you'd like to discuss is inefficient and can even be annoying.

Instead, build the confidence to be upfront about what you want without being rude.

Again, *without being rude*.

I've seen too many examples of people saying, "I tell it like it is. If they don't like it, that's their problem."

While I love the confidence, I've seen students time and again say something offensive for the sake of brevity that ends up burning a bridge, causing a fight, or getting them into more trouble later. What they thought would save time actually ends up taking a lot more time in the long run because of added drama.

An example of clarity might take place during a group project. A student leader might say something like this to a group member who is behind:

*"(Name), I know you want to get a good grade on this project – we do too. I also understand how busy you are with school right now. Do you think it's reasonable for you to get your part of the project to us by Thursday of next week?"*

This way, the leader has opened up a dialogue while being clear about a deadline.

However, there are lots and lots of students out there who would not approach the situation like this.

Some students wouldn't say anything, and we all know what this means – it means they are about to do the entire project.

Other students would jump in and say, *"Is there anything I can do to help?"*

The issue with this question is the same as not saying anything at all – it usually ends with the ambitious student doing the entire project on behalf of their team.[10]

True student leaders are upfront about expectations and objectives from the start of a project, and they communicate these expectations thoroughly to a group so they don't get stuck doing all the work.

Clarity takes practice and patience.

Have you ever said something that didn't come out the way you had planned it? Me too.

It has happened to everyone, even these prestigious student leaders I talk so much about.

The difference is that student leaders will take a scenario in which they weren't as clear as they could have been, think back to it and *analyze* it – through this analysis, they will determine ways they can think about the scenario differently in the future to be more clear the next time a similar scenario comes up.[11]

## Be Polite

This might seem obvious, but it has become clear to me and many other experts that it is anything but obvious in our current world.

It's something even adults forget (as you may have noticed).

Adults with esteemed jobs have been fired or suffered ruined reputations because they have made inappropriate comments.

---

[10] And adding a whole lot of stress to an already stressful life.

[11] Think back to the *Analysis* section of the Action Packed Leadership framework on page 14: *Thoughts, Actions, Outcomes, Analysis.*

**Stay away from hurtful remarks regarding disability, race, gender, sexual orientation, or ethnicity.**

I cannot stress this enough. Your intentions of a comment as a harmless joke won't matter to those you have offended by it.

Remember, your *thoughts* alone don't make you a better person – your *behavior* does.

If your behavior stems from your thoughts, it is important to dig deep to see if you hold any subconscious or conscious prejudices or biases towards other people.

This is simply a practice in *self-awareness*.

If, deep down, you hold some type of bias or ill-will toward another person or group, you will need to do your best to ask yourself a lot of questions about this bias and work on defusing it internally before putting your thoughts verbally into the world. There is no space for prejudice if your cup is filled with kindness, compassion, and love.

We're simply focusing on verbal communication at this very moment, but I'm sure you can think of other places people could check their biases and be a little bit nicer to each other.

Aside from the obvious harm you could do with impolite or inappropriate comments, student leaders also know the value politeness and appropriate comments can bring.

Misery is not the only thing that loves company. *Enthusiasm also loves company.*

When you are bright and polite, the world will treat you the same way. To get it right – be bright and polite.

### Increase Your Vocabulary

Improving your vocabulary will allow you to better communicate with peers and connect with professionals in your desired field. It will also help you remove those, *like*, useless filler words that *–um* – distract from your ideas and personality, *y'know?*

# ACTION PACKED LEADERSHIP

Just one word of caution: *know your audience.*

> **PRO TIP #1**
>
> In the inside cover of books you read either for class or leisure, write down any word you don't know and look it up when you have some time.

Using your newfound vocabulary when hanging with friends could be seen as presumptuous[12]; doing so when making a speech to adults may be effective.

## NONVERBAL COMMUNICATION

Now that we've discussed how to use your *voice*, I think it is equally as important to mention that a majority of communication is what *isn't* said.

More often than not, it is explained like this:

> **QUOTABLE:**
>
> *"As a student, nonverbal communication is something I see my peers struggle with every day. A lot of it comes along with attitude."*
>
> —LYNN TOMLINSON
> FORMER MICHIGAN FCCLA VICE PRESIDENT OF MEMBERSHIP

It's not just what you say, but how you say it. UCLA psychologist Albert Mehrabian conducted a study, which revealed that communication is:

» 55% body/facial
» 38% tone/pitch
» 7% verbal

Nonverbal communication comprises a majority of how we receive a message!! (Mehrabian, 1967)

---

[12] **Pre·sump·tu·ous** adjective (of a person or their behavior) *failing to observe the limits of what is permitted or appropriate.*
I gave you the first one, but use PRO TIP #1 for any other words that might make you say, "huh?"

I often tell people to grab a partner and say the following phrases to each other while actually trying to convey the opposite of each message.

You can try it too. Try to say the words below, but, with your tone and facial expressions, put a sarcastic or negative spin to each one.

» You look good today

» That jacket is really pretty

» Do you believe you can achieve big things?

**FYI**

Communication is:
55% body/facial
38% tone/pitch
7% verbal

I think you'll see pretty quickly that your tone, pitch, facial expressions, and body movements can completely change the meaning of your words.

It amazes me that more students are not frequently evaluating their nonverbal cues. Nonverbal communication allows you to reinforce what is said in words, convey emotions, and provide feedback to others.

### Reinforce What is Said in Words

If you say, "I'm excited to attend your event" with a roll of your eyes and a shrug of your shoulders, you will appear insincere.[13]

But if you say this brightly with a smile and eye contact, your nonverbal communication will reinforce your intended message.

This has everything to do with *saying* what you *mean*.

When you mean what you say, your nonverbals should naturally reflect your words.

If you haven't noticed, the entire goal is to shape your thoughts so they consistently upgrade your actions.

---

[13] Feel free to try this. Say, "I'm excited to attend your event" while rolling your eyes and shrugging your shoulders and see if you can make it sound sincere – I bet you can't.

The actions you begin to take are not simply for the sake of taking action – your actions should become *effortless* based on who you are (and who you are becoming).

## Convey Emotions

Be animated! You don't want others to read boredom or lack of interest on your face.

One of the biggest struggles for high school students today is the perceived need to be nonchalant about everything.

We all know that student who is constantly too cool to participate in anything. There were a few of these guys on the high school basketball team I told you about.

It's okay to get excited. To exhibit energy. To laugh until you cry. These aren't flaws. They are actually endearing and will make others want to be around your energy.

## Feedback

Nodding your head or giving a vocal affirmation such as "mmhmm" shows your interest and investment in the speaker.

I'm sure you've seen someone take his or her phone out while someone else is talking and say, *"Keep going. I'm listening."*

The truth is, this person is not listening. Everything in their body language contradicts what they said. The nonverbal feedback this person is giving says more than their words can.

*Student leaders make eye contact, listen well, and are engaged when others talk.*

Noticing these nonverbal signals in others can benefit you as well.

The practice of recognizing the nonverbal gestures of someone else fits within the realm of emotional intelligence (or EQ) – a subset of why *thoughts* are the primary focus of this book.

If you're able to think about and *understand* the positive or negative vibes you're getting from others, you can shift your style of communication to fit the needs of those with whom you are communicating.

A few quick tips concerning this practice:

Watch for eye contact, tone of voice, and eyebrows – if eyebrows are up, interest is up; when eyebrows are down, interest is waning. If you see your listeners losing interest, try a different approach to capture attention (Horn, 2012).

### PRO TIP #2

Know the Eyebrow Code.
**Eyebrows up** = interested.
**Eyebrows furrowed** = confused.
**Eyebrows unmoved** = not interested.
*Watch people's eyebrows when you speak – it'll make you a more effective communicator.*

Use these nonverbal skills as you lead and communicate with others.

I'd like you to picture yourself inviting students to a meeting into which you have put time and energy. When you start giving details of the meeting, your listeners drift off. They start to break eye contact, get their phones out, or start to whisper to one another.

What do you do?

This is your cue – instead of continuing to present the information as you were, use your new-found emotional intelligence to switch your style. Maybe touch on a few different topics to see what catches their attention.

If you notice their eyebrows instantly perk up when you mention PIZZA will be at the meeting, this is a topic to which you may want to devote a little more time.[14]

---

[14] Your mouth may have just started watering with the mention of pizza – I'll understand if you take a quick snack break before continuing to read.

Pizza may not be the purpose of your meeting, but if it succeeds in getting more people to attend, you've achieved your goal.

The following is a chart to help you navigate the world of nonverbal communication.

Watch for these gestures in your own and others' communication.

### EYES:

SMALL PUPILS = concentration
LARGE PUPILS = tuning out
NARROW EYES = intensity or anger
EYE CONTACT = interest
SHIFTING EYES = disinterest
ROLLING EYES = disagreement

### HANDS AND ARMS:

FIST = aggression or anger
HAND TO CHIN = concentration
POINTED FINGER = threatening
ARMS TIGHTLY FOLDED = disagreement
HANDS ON HIPS = authority
HANDS UP AND OPEN = pleading
FIDGETING = nervousness

### MOUTH:

TIGHT LIPS = anger
OPEN MOUTH = wonder or astonishment
SMILE = happiness
FROWN = sadness
CROOKED SMILE = doubt

### SHOULDERS:

SLOUCH = tired or weary
CHEST OUT = pride
SHOULDERS BACK = confidence
TIGHT ABDOMEN = prepared
LEANING FORWARD = interest
LEANING AWAY = disinterest

### HEAD:

TILTED = caring
HELD HIGH = confidence or pride
CHIN TO CHEST = aggression
ROLLED BACK = disgust or defeat
NODDING = agreement or understanding
SIDE TO SIDE = disagreement

### LEGS AND FEET:

CONSTANT MOVEMENT/TAPPING = nervous
LEGS CROSSED = relaxed or casual

Nonverbal communication can change the emotional temperature of a room.

What do your nonverbal signals say about you when you walk into the room?

I'll give you a chance to answer questions like this one at the end of this chapter.

---

**Confidence:**
*"Never be overwhelmed by the moment. Acting like you've "been there" before helps you avoid looking like an amateur and demands respect. Finding the balance between looking cocky and looking like a deer caught in the headlights takes time, but when found, the right amount of confidence will be invaluable in successful relationships."*

—Mike Seely
Former Washington DECA State President

---

## LISTENING IS THAT IMPORTANT

Another section on listening?

Yes. It is THAT important – and there are a few more things you need to know.

Knowing how to step back and hear your peers' ideas is an essential aspect of communication. An effective leader is one that takes charge while also giving others a chance to voice their opinions.

But here's the important part:

It's not just about the *act* of listening. It is about *actually* listening.

Again, this is a paradigm shift in how people tend to think.

Most people think:

*"If I hear you, that's enough."*

I'd encourage you to think:

*"Truly listening is an act of mental openness and understanding – my ability to listen well is 100% based in my thoughts."*

When asked about this concept, international speaker and best-selling author, Jake Kelfer, told me how important it is that young people take a genuine interest in others. He said, "Ideally, all you thought you were doing originally was asking questions because you were genuinely interested in listening to what another person had to say. What you ended up doing was laying the foundation for a fantastic relationship. Don't underestimate the power of asking questions and being a good listener."

Listening isn't just valuable because it makes *others* feel heard – it is valuable because it gives *you* ideas. You may pick up new thoughts and perspectives you didn't have already.

I still talk to students all the time who think they listen well but can't tell me one scenario in which they decided to go with someone else's idea over theirs. True listening means being open to potential outcomes that were not your idea.

Listening takes *thought* – to truly listen, student leaders need to let go of their own egos and **to really, truly and wholeheartedly, believe in the value of others.** This mental practice is hard. It means letting go of any bias or stubbornness – any preconceived notions or previously generated ideas. It means opening your eyes to the fact that everyone has something to share, and just maybe, someone else's ideas may be just as good, if not better, than yours. Real leaders look to create a balance between their vision and a shared vision.

The more you decide to look at the *thoughts* behind the *actions*, the more successful you will be in the long run. Listening is not simply a physical task – it is an act of *mindful leadership*.

## MOTION CREATES EMOTION

Someone I've always respected used to say, *"Motion creates emotion."*

When we start to move, we begin to change.

This concept is backed by science. In his bestselling book, *Money: Master the Game*, Tony Robbins cites studies that show even changing something as small as your posture for two minutes can be a game changer in your life.

Striking a more powerful position for two minutes has the ability to increase testosterone (the *dominance* hormone) by 25% and decrease cortisol (the *stress* hormone) by 20%.

Again, these numbers are after just **two minutes**!

Can you imagine being 20% less stressed in just two minutes?

Imagine what could happen if you begin making physical adjustments every day.

I tell you this because, at times, we need to first take *action* and our *thoughts* will follow.

Yes, I understand if you just said, "Doesn't that contradict the chart you showed us earlier in the book?" (Thoughts, Actions, Outcomes, Analysis).

The truth is, sometimes your first thought needs to be:

*I need to take one action.*

You don't have to have all your thoughts figured out before taking the first step – this is the classic mistake of *overthinking*. Most often, our thoughts begin to come together once we've taken some sort of initial action. And if we've already determined our values (as you learned earlier) your first action will typically be a good one.

It is for this reason that teachers around the country recommend students go for a short walk or jog in the morning before taking the ACT exam. The initial *action* can fuel a higher level of *thought*.

However, the model on page 14 (Thoughts, Actions, Outcomes, Analysis) still applies – the only shift is in your first thought:

*I need to take one action.*

You are not putting action before thought entirely – you are simply encouraging your first thought to get you to take action.

In this way, if you ever find your actions are not naturally following your thoughts ("I wanted to get out of bed and go to school, but I just couldn't get up"), you'll need to push yourself to take *one action* to get yourself going, and from there it will get easier to take the proper actions moving forward.

This *take action* framework can improve your communication skills by leaps and bounds.

Specifically, from a listening perspective, below are some ways you can reverse the model and allow your initial *actions* to dictate your future *thoughts*.

*Show* a speaker you are listening through your *actions* by:

- Making eye contact
- Nodding
- Asking questions
- Not interrupting

> **QUOTABLE:**
>
> *"The most important thing in communication is hearing what isn't said."*
>
> – PETER DRUCKER

Notice that listening does not simply involve what is being *said*. There are plenty of nonverbal cues to be aware of both when you are speaking as well as when you are the listener.

For example, if you notice another student rolling his eyes while you're speaking during a Student Council meeting, be aware that he is probably not happy with what you are saying. Address this situation by asking for his opinion or confronting him individually after the meeting.

Important note: AFTER THE MEETING.

Bringing his actions up in front of an entire group may alienate him and make him less apt to follow you in the future. Waiting too long may cause the situation to grow.

Of course, this type of confrontation after a meeting should still be done from a place of kindness – keeping a Student Council member after a meeting to tell him what he did wrong will not help the situation. It is better to ask how he was feeling or if he had thoughts about what was covered and listen well to what he has to say.

Everyone has something different to offer. Student leaders recognize that they aren't the only ones with good ideas, and they open up discussion before making final decisions.

## CHRISTMAS CARDS IN JULY (TEXTING)

One of my biggest pet peeves when talking with people is when they get their phone out and say, "Keep going. I'm listening." I usually proceed to tell them what I was saying only for them to look back up from their phone and say, "Can you say that again? I'm sorry."

When you send text messages while you're engaged in face-to-face conversations, you're letting the person you're with know what's on your phone is more interesting than what they have to say.

Frankly, it's rude.

To communicate well, put your phone away and look people in the eye. If you must have your phone out, step to the side, send your message, and then reengage with whomever you're talking to. It is appropriate to say, "I apologize, I need to answer this quickly then I'll put my phone away."

**FYI**

On average, teens check their phones 60 times a day to text, check social media, play games and listen to music.

**(PewResearch)**

A former mentor of mine, Father John Naus, was the type of person who would send Christmas cards in July. He would personally deliver balloon animals to people just because. He wore an ever-present smile on his face, and if you looked directly at him, it was impossible to miss the twinkle in his eyes. I think I'd go so far as to say he was the happiest person I've ever come into contact with – and his happiness radiated into the world in waves of positive energy; waves so big and so bright that I don't even believe he knew the ripple effect he was creating.

He lived his entire life in service to other people. He laughed with them, cried with them, and grew old with them. If you needed to find Father Naus, you could just find him. It wasn't difficult. You didn't have to send a text or e-mail. You didn't have to wonder where he was, and I truly believe this was because if you needed something, whether he knew you were looking for him or not, in his heart he was already looking for you.

John Naus passed away in 2013 at the age of 89.

At his funeral, kind words about Father Naus could be heard echoing through the packed church. Stories about his life were being shared through the kind of happy tears you only get at the funeral of someone who had lived well.

There was one phrase Father Naus had used in his life that kept coming up. It was repeated through the pews and into the aisles; it filled the sidewalks outside, and it drove home in the minds of everyone who attended.

Father John Naus would always say, "See written on the forehead of every person you meet, 'Make me feel important.'"

And boy, did he do a good job of that.

This mantra has never been more necessary.

Make people feel important. When you're with them, put your phone away. When you text them, remember they can't hear your tone or pitch and be extra careful not to come across the wrong way.

Texting can be a great short-form way to stay connected or get brief messages across. Utilize it, but do not let it distract you from living in the present and giving away your attention like you have an unlimited supply — I promise you, if you give all your attention to others today, you'll have more attention to give away tomorrow.

Everyone wants to feel like they are receiving the attention they deserve, and giving this attention helps student leaders build strong relationships with those they are lucky enough to serve.

> *See written on the forehead of every person you meet, 'Make Me Feel Important.'*
>
> Fr. John Naus[15]

## CHECKING YOUR INBOX

Aside from face-to-face communication, e-mail is the primary means of communication in the working world. Use it to efficiently communicate among individuals and teams. Student leaders follow these guidelines when using e-mail:

### Name

Create a professional e-mail account with which you are comfortable associating yourself. Get rid of the middle-school "crazy4soccer" account, and instead use your first and last name so it is easy for others to identify you[16]. Colleges and potential employers will take you more seriously, too.

### Respond Promptly

Check your e-mail at least once a day. People expect e-mails to be checked often, and not responding promptly can be interpreted as disinterest or rudeness. As a rule of thumb, respond to e-mails

---

[15] Father John Naus was a Jesuit professor of philosophy at Marquette University (my alma mater) for nearly half a century. He was known for his love of humor, Christmas cards, and balloon animals. He died in September of 2013, but not before touching the lives of thousands (including mine).

[16] For example, kyle.willkom@gmail.com is a professional e-mail address — feel free to send me an e-mail if you are seeing this.

within 24 hours, even if the response simply lets the sender know you will get back to them at a future time.

### Address Correctly

How you address an e-mail matters: "Hey" and "Hi!" are friendly and informal greetings. In a formal e-mail, use "Dear _____," or simply their name: "Professor Stewart." Double-check the recipient's title; do not address someone as Mrs. if they are unmarried (then it would be Ms.); address a professor who has a Ph.D. as "Dr." unless they indicate otherwise. If someone with a Ph.D. says, "Call me Steve," it is appropriate to call him Steve.

### Past Interaction

It's easy to overlook or forget about old e-mails. Any important information you are given via e-mail should be written down or documented elsewhere: give yourself a phone reminder or copy it into your agenda or calendar. This sounds easy, but very few students stay disciplined enough to keep information organized. You will separate yourself as a leader when this becomes second nature.

**PRO TIP #3**

If you have a smart phone, manage your e-mail settings so you can check e-mail at your convenience.

### Clarity

E-mail is meant to be a concise way to get a message across. It loses the ability to be useful if a personal conversation could be shorter and clearer. Be concise in e-mails and consider making a phone call if the e-mail becomes too lengthy.

### Begin with What You Want

You are more likely to get a response if you clearly state your purpose in the first sentence. Feel free to expand in the following sentences, but being up-front with what you are looking for saves your reader time. Too many students start an e-mail with, "I hope you're doing well." Leave this to the end of the e-mail.

An example of an effective e-mail lead:

"Dear James, I'm wondering if you could volunteer at my event this Friday evening at 7:00 PM." This lets James know exactly what you're looking for. Explain in the following sentences what your event is, where it is, and why you think he should volunteer, and feel free to end with pleasantries like, "I hope you are doing well."

### Never E-mail Out of Anger (Ever, Ever, Ever)

If you're upset about something, separate yourself from the issue before saying something damaging. Abide by the 24-hour rule: if you are still upset about something a full day later, it may be appropriate to calmly and respectfully address your problem. If the problem seems smaller, it's likely all you needed was time. Take a moment to stop and breathe before sending anything you may regret.

### Review

Although most means of digital communication are informal, e-mail is not. Lack of capitalization, misspellings, and loose punctuation rules should not be applied to e-mails. Use full sentences, proper grammar, and check for spelling. And always double-check the recipients – there's nothing more embarrassing than accidentally sending a snarky e-mail meant for your friends to your principal.

E-mail can be used for a variety of situations. It is appropriate to e-mail teammates inviting them to a pasta dinner before a game. It is polite to send a follow up email after a job interview to thank them for their time (although a hand-written thank you note is far better). You can also use e-mail to reach out to potential employers and establish contacts for the future. Be careful to follow the guidelines outlined above when utilizing e-mail as your communication tool.

## FRUIT-SHAPED SOAP (SOCIAL MEDIA)

When I was a sophomore in college, I had an interview for an internship at a technology startup.

Before asking any questions or engaging in any small talk, my interviewers, Matt and Kris, informed me they didn't have any internship positions open at the moment. I was a little disheartened and wondered why they had asked me to interview at all.

I kept my head up as the interview officially began. I answered questions the best I could, even though I was certain there would be no internship offer for me that day.

At the end of the interview, Matt and Kris said I should keep in touch with them on Twitter about future opportunities. It seems crazy to me now, but at the time, I didn't even have a Twitter account – which I meekly let them know.

They proceeded to tell me why Twitter was one of their favorite social media platforms – they mentioned following people who share interests, interacting with people I normally wouldn't have a chance to connect with, and learning how other people *think* (which I'm sure you could guess from me writing this book – learning how other people think was high on my priority list).

They even pulled out a computer and started giving me examples, "Let's say you were interested in something kind of crazy…like fruit-shaped soap – we can instantly find people on Twitter who post about fruit-shaped soap!"

I created a Twitter account (@KyleWillkom) as soon as I got home, clicked the "Follow" button on Matt and Kris, and responded often to their posts.

Fortunately for me, this story has a happy ending other than me creating my first Twitter account.

Six months later, an internship opportunity opened up at their company – and guess who was at the top of their hiring list.

Shortly after the position opened up, I was walking into their office for my first day as an intern, and it wouldn't have been possible without social media.

I can also confidently say that I wouldn't be where I am today if not for the guidance and opportunities provided by Matt and Kris.

Social media has become a necessary means of connecting with others. It can be used to enhance your well-being, make connections, develop your personal brand, and push projects forward.

Social media can also help you reach a larger audience with less effort.

If you are working towards a cause – putting together a creative video and sharing it on YouTube is an awesome way to spread the word.

If you are in charge of organizing something, creating an event on Facebook and inviting friends is a great idea. Build up buzz by following this up with tweets, texts, phone calls, and in-person conversations.

As with any platform, student leaders must be careful to use social media as a productive tool. Posting with bad language, inappropriate content, or messages that don't align with your personal brand (which you'll read about in the next chapter) can have a negative effect on your credibility.

As with e-mail, review things you post, and ask yourself if this is something with which you would like to be associated.

Avoid putting anyone down or getting into online debates that aren't fruitful.

Keep in mind your online footprint will follow you forever. Yes, forever. Your grandchildren will someday be able to look back and review your entire life online. Scary, huh? Make sure they like what they see.

• • •

As a student leader and beyond, communication is key.

The tips you read about in this chapter will help you convey your ideas and take the first step toward being a strong young leader. Take these tips with you as you move forward in this book, and understand the way you communicate is synonymous with the way you *think*.

Your communication on any platform or via any medium is intertwined with your *values, character,* and *identity*. So whether you are an expert communicator or just starting to think about it, I'd encourage you to begin filling your cup from the bottom with desirable contents. If it is true that from the abundance of the heart the mouth speaks, do your best every day to fill your heart with gratitude, joy, patience, generosity, kindness, and love. Your communication style will see a seismic shift.

These lessons on communication are intertwined with every other lesson you'll see moving forward – in every *action* there is first *thought*. Keep this in mind as we continue to dive into the mind of a leader.

## **CHAPTER 1** ACTION PACKED DISCUSSION QUESTIONS

*1. What are two specific ways you can improve your communication skills?*

*2. Which nonverbal cues do you pick up on the most? Which do you feel are the most important?*

*3. What are three ineffective ways students communicate?*

*4. What can you do to ensure you are communicating well on social media?*

Chapter 2 Preface
# THE DECA GUY

In the making of this book, I had the opportunity to connect with successful student leaders from around the country. I had phone calls with them, asked them questions after my talks, surveyed them on social media, and e-mailed back and forth with them about the topics in this book.

I learned a great deal from all of them, and each one had a different perspective that helped shape this book into what it is.

When it comes to personal branding, one student in particular stood out to me.

By his sophomore year at the University of Missouri Kansas City, Jaspreet became the Twitter voice of the Kansas City Airport as well as an intern at United Airlines.

I asked Jaspreet about his journey to becoming a successful student leader and as he responded it became more and more clear to me – it wasn't just about what he was *doing*; it was about who he *was*.

The decisions Jaspreet made much earlier in his life set him up for success in college. His passions, dedication, and work ethic made him the ideal candidate for both positions at such a young age.

Jaspreet had been passionate about the airline industry his whole life. He knew early on being in the airline industry was the direction he wanted to go, but he wasn't exactly sure how to get there. He knew every type of commercial plane and could tell you interesting things about each model. The airline industry was simply something Jaspreet *loved*.

Understanding a passion is one thing – finding the success Jaspreet has found is another.

Jaspreet's journey started by getting involved in a student organization as a clueless high school freshman.

"My DECA partner my freshman year of high school pretty much forced me to compete. I had to write a 30-page plan and I didn't really know what I was doing at that point. But my DECA partner and my advisor really engaged me and helped me along the way."

Jaspreet got more and more involved. He started seeing the DECA organization as his pathway to personal and professional success.

"In high school, I became known as 'The DECA Guy.' Writing that plan as a freshman, by the time I was a senior, I knew business plans inside and out. I knew how to put them together, and I actually launched a couple companies while I was still in high school...I also became the State Reporter for DECA my junior year and the State President my senior year."

It was only a matter of time before Jaspreet was able to mesh his business knowledge and experience with the industry that he had always loved – the airline industry.

"I think it was my DECA experience and how actively involved I got that made a huge difference in the long run. Doing that back then definitely helped me get to where I am now."

THE DECA GUY  55

This chapter is all about how you are perceived and what you are known for.

Jaspreet became known as "The DECA Guy." It was simply how people saw him based on the actions he took.

Lucky for Jaspreet, DECA is an organization with over 200,000 members that pushes the ideals of being academically-prepared, community-oriented, professionally-responsible and experienced leaders. He probably didn't think about it at the time, but being "The DECA Guy" automatically associated him with these ideal traits.

As "The DECA Guy," he was, in the minds of those around him, the living example of an academically-prepared, community-oriented, professionally-responsible, experienced leader.

Talk about a personal brand!

By creating his personal brand early on, Jaspreet was able to obtain two great internships by his sophomore year of college.

He has gone on to work full-time for United Airlines as a Product Analyst and spends his weekends up in the air – traveling to new and interesting locations.

Because of the building blocks he put into place early in his life, as of the writing of this book, Jaspreet has flown around the world 22 times!!

You can follow Jaspreet's travels on Instagram and Twitter at @Jaspreettravels.

In this chapter, I'll talk about:

- Making the personal brand decision
- Dressing the part
- Personal branding on social media

Let's do it.

Chapter 2
# PERSONAL BRANDING

*"We are the CEOs of our own companies: Me Inc. Our most important job is to be head marketer for the brand called You."*

—Tom Peters, Fast Company

When you see a Nike swoosh, what comes to mind?

Some may say athleticism, diligence, and strength. I'm sure Nike would like to align itself with these ideals.

Some may say uncomfortable, expensive, or overrated. Obviously, Nike wouldn't be as happy with these reviews.

Companies purposefully work to establish positive associations in the minds of consumers. If they didn't, who would buy their products? Through advertising, marketing, and outreach, businesses do everything they can to get to our thoughts, feelings, and emotions in the right ways.

It is often overlooked that, similar to a company like Nike, you can do this too!

Everyone in the world has a *personal brand.*

**A personal brand is simply the thoughts, feelings, and emotions other people have when they think about you.**

A personal brand allows you to let others know *who you are* and *what you stand for.*

Personal brands aren't just for celebrities and politicians – as a student, you can brand yourself as a leader, college applicant, or responsible employee.

There are actions you can take to become known for one thing or another – just as Jaspreet became known as "The DECA Guy."

Your brand includes things such as your attitude, personality, image, appearance, and online presence.

Keep in mind, as with communication, personal branding is not simply about *doing* the right things, but *being* the right person.

Tomorrow, a senior girl could wake up and say, "Today, I'm going to be nice to everyone because I want them to vote for me to be prom queen."

Do you think one day of kindness will influence other students to vote for her more than the way she treated people every other day of her high school career? Personally, I think it's unlikely.[17]

Our consistent actions define us. The things we do day in and day out will tell others more about who we are than a standalone moment ever could.

I sometimes think about Jaspreet's interviews with United Airlines. How refreshing do you think it was for the hiring manager to sit down across from someone who had a lifelong love of the airline industry?

Anyone could look up United Airlines the night before an interview and get some basic facts, but I can just picture Jaspreet holding a

---

[17] Unless her one day of kindness also included giving every student who voted for her $100. She could probably get some votes then.

fascinating in-depth conversation during an internship interview about the difference between an Airbus A319 and an Airbus A320.

I have no idea if this conversation actually happened, but I'd be willing to bet Jaspreet was a no-brainer hire for United Airlines – I am certain they could easily see *who* he was and *what he cared about* in just a short amount of time because of the actions he consistently took each day of his life.

Unfortunately, there is some bad news.

The world does not always simply reward positive action. You can do all the right things and still not get the results you're looking for. Recently, I pulled over and parked my car to help try to catch a lost dog that had escaped from a little girl's leash. I ran after this dog for three-and-a-half miles only to lose sight of it behind a house and have to walk back to my car disappointed, hoping the dog would be found soon. True story.

Things don't always go our way.

The same is true with a personal brand.

When it comes to personal branding, you don't always have control of what other people think of you.

In our quick-response world, people are always going to judge you without knowing you first. It is the reason people will tell you first impressions are lasting impressions. Even studies discussed in Forbes Magazine have shown interviewers decide on whether they will hire someone or not in the first *seven seconds* of meeting them.

Seven seconds!! That's about enough time for, "Hi, nice to meet you" and a handshake.

Seem unfair? It is.

But there is good news.

Are you ready for it?[18]

---

[18] Anytime I say, "Are you ready for it?" I instantly think of the Taylor Swift song.

You can heavily influence these snap judgments based on simple decisions. You contribute to your personal brand – or how others will perceive you – every single day based on *who* you are and *what you stand for*.

You can mold your brand any way you wish. You can make decisions about how you would like to be viewed by your peers and future employers (or employees if you start your own business), then you can create actions around those desires.

Take a moment to think of the positive words others might already use to describe you. What are some adjectives your closest friends might say to describe you in the best possible way? There are most likely some awesome reasons behind why people would describe you with these words.

Now take a moment to think of your worst enemies – people who dislike you, ignore you, or don't give you the time of day. What are some of the negative words these people might use to describe you? Are there reasons they say these things or are they completely unfounded?

I promise I don't ask you this to get you upset, sad, or angry. I simply ask you to look at both sides of the coin to think about the following questions:

» How can I continue to build the positive attributes of my personal brand? What actions can I take?

» If there are legitimate reasons for people to use a negative adjective to describe me, are there actions I can take to change these perceptions?

These questions fit within the central theme of this book – *thinking* about these questions is great, but *taking action* surrounding these questions will lead to a shift in your personal brand or the thoughts, feelings, and emotions people have about you.

What words or qualities make up your personal brand?

As a Senior at Sumner High School in Washington, Student Body President Nick Yochum told me his school focuses on 8 positive qualities saying, "If you're consistently able to practice these 8 qualities and put them into action, you'll be able to build influence in your school."

The 8 qualities are: patience, kindness, respectfulness, humility, selflessness, forgiveness, honesty, and commitment.[19]

Sumner High School has built a framework to help students establish a leadership-focused personal brand – but it is on each student to make the decision to boldly put these adjectives into practice.

Some other positive words that can make up a personal brand might include:

- Artistic
- Adventurous
- Athletic
- Funny
- Happy
- Interesting
- Involved
- Kind
- Motivated
- Organized
- Professional
- Responsible
- Smart
- Thoughtful

Do any of these describe you? Are there actions you can take to allow others to see these qualities in you more?

Some negative words that could be used to describe a personal brand might be:

- Arrogant
- High-maintenance
- Ignorant
- Insensitive
- Lazy
- Negative
- Rude
- Unhappy

Could any of these currently be used to describe you? Are there actions you can take to shift these negatives into the positives listed just before?

---

[19] He also told me a great way to remember these 8 qualities is to use the phrase, "Pink kittens have red socks for Halloween costumes." See if you can commit these qualities to memory now.

All of this is also to say – if you are being bullied in any way, called names, or ridiculed, *you do not deserve it*. If people are describing you in negative ways for no reason at all, please tell an adult. If you are someone who judges others unfairly, please stop. The world already has enough mean people; you don't need to be one.

Choose positive words to identify yourself, and work to eliminate negative images of yourself in your everyday life.

Personal branding is not fitting into a cookie-cutter mold of what others want you to be. Everyone is different.

Do you want to be known as athletic, responsible, and motivated?

Interesting, artistic, and smart?

Happy, thoughtful, and kind?

Decide for yourself, and start filling your cup from the bottom – take positive action *everyday* towards the adjectives you best identify with.[20]

## FAKE IT UNTIL YOU MAKE IT? THEN WHAT?

Throughout my life I've grown hyper-aware of all the bad advice in the world.

It is everywhere.

You could probably turn on Netflix and hear some bad advice in about five seconds.

If you don't think you've gotten any bad advice, it's most likely because you're following it.

Bad advice disguises itself as good advice at every turn – that's why people give it. Companies try to give advice on what to purchase, how to dress, what medications to take, and the list goes on and on.

---

[20] Pro tip: if you don't know what actions to take, start asking questions. The more questions you ask of trustworthy people the more answers you tend to get.

One piece of advice I've always wrestled with is, "Fake it until you make it." My natural tendency to question everything always led me to ask, "What happens when I do make it?"

Have you ever felt like you are in over your head? Like you've been placed in a position you were not prepared for? Have you felt that knot in your stomach as if you forgot your lines in a play, didn't know the answer when called on, or couldn't remember the notes you're supposed to play at a piano recital?

I've felt that knot in my stomach more than once, and to be honest, I wish I could tell you that I had a way for you to avoid this feeling for the rest of your life. I don't think such a way exists.

However, I can tell you that there is a better phrase to sum up what you're trying to do.

Fake it until you *become* it.

There is absolutely nothing wrong with dressing nicer than you normally would for your first day of an internship. There is nothing wrong with trying to speak the language of an industry you're looking to get into before you have much experience in it. There is nothing wrong with pushing yourself to engage in conversations or experiences outside of your comfort zone.

However, if you are simply doing so to try to gain a job, money, or notoriety – if you are being someone you're not to get the attention of a girl or guy you think is cute – if you have no intention of being the person you are presenting to others – you will find that the knot in your stomach will continue to grow. You will constantly feel out of place. You won't know how to act or what to say. You'll feel this way because you have chosen a path that doesn't allow yourself to be *authentically you.*

*Fulfillment is much easier to find when it is truly and uniquely you who is looking for it.* If you are chasing someone else's dream, you may achieve an immense amount of success, but it won't feel like your success. It will feel like theirs. You have to be the captain of your own ship.

I say "Fake it until you *become* it" because it leaves room for you to become the *best version of yourself*.

If you just want to *make it*, you may find your life heading in a direction you didn't ask for.

If you take time to *think* about your personal brand and put yourself in positions to *become* it, you'll be moving towards a *perceived identity* that matches your *true identity*.

When it comes to a personal brand, this is exactly what you want to happen.

Through *thoughts* and *actions* backed by desirable *values*, we build *character* and create a *true identity* for ourselves – who we are when no one's watching.

## QUOTABLE:

*"4-H was my passion. My home. So I kept working at it. My only goal was to be a good example for younger 4-H members. I was hoping my story would encourage members to believe in themselves and not give up. I lost 3 or 4 times before I won any type of position, but I kept trying because it was my passion. I hope others can find an organization like that."*

— WILL DALTON
FORMER TN 4-H STATE COUNCIL PRESIDENT

When our *perceived identity* – the way others would describe us – matches our *true identity*, we have developed a strong *personal brand*.

When student leaders fill their cups from the bottom, they begin the process in the right place – with themselves.

This way, when the storm of bad advice comes rolling in and the winds of distraction start to push you off course, your compass will continue to point towards exactly where you're wanting to go.

The funny part about this difference in terminology – fake it until you make it vs. fake it until you *become* it – is how others begin to respond.

Student leaders who are working to *become the best version of themselves* receive help in scenarios where they might be pushed out of their comfort zone. People will have their back, even if it looks like they may fail. People do this because they know the *behavior* is coming from a good place – that the student leader wants to improve, learn, and grow.

When it appears that the *behavior* is not coming from a good place, people don't want to help anymore. When it appears a young person is being self-centered, egotistical, or unintentional, the help of others will fade away.

It is okay to change your behavior based on the scenario you find yourself in, so long as you are also working to *become* the person you are acting like – this way, you are never straying from being truly and authentically you.

## ARE YOU A MESS OR DO YOU KNOW HOW TO DRESS?

Superficial as it may be, we humans make assessments about people by their appearances constantly. Dressing appropriately is vital in creating your brand. The beauty of a personal brand is that it is unique to each individual; a professional athlete and a businessman or woman are not expected to dress similarly.

Ask yourself if your attire is cohesive with the personal brand you are looking to build, and follow these basic guidelines:

### Be Ready

No matter your area of interest, it's a good idea to have one professional outfit on hand for an important meeting or interview. A shirt, tie, and dress shoes are a wardrobe staple in most professional settings. A dress may also be fitting for women in a professional setting.

### Be Neat

Looking dirty, disheveled, and messy is distracting and can turn people off. No matter your personal style, try to appear clean and hygienic.

QUOTABLE:

*"Dress shabbily and they remember the dress. Dress impeccably and they remember the woman."*

–COCO CHANEL
(THIS APPLIES TO GUYS TOO.)

### Know Your Environment

What you wear to an interview, to class, and to a concert will be different. Your brand is always being developed – even outside the classroom or office. Use common sense to assess what's appropriate. Images of you on social media, even in casual environments, should not harm your personal brand.

### Be Appropriate

Generally, stay away from clothing that contains offensive or suggestive graphics, is revealing, skin-tight, or wrinkled. This applies across genders.

### Show Some Personality

Make yourself stand out. Do you have a favorite tie? A bright colored belt? A favorite statement necklace? What you wear will be the first thing most people notice and judge about you. Portray yourself in a way in which people will remember you. Keep in mind – you want their memory of you to also align with your personal brand. Standing out just for the sake of standing out is not helpful to you.

### Confidence

It doesn't matter what adjectives you choose to be staples of your personal brand – the idea is however you choose to be or look, always be confident in yourself. Wear your favorite blazer or wear those shoes that make you feel like a million bucks. The idea is that you own the style you choose.

## BUILDING YOUR BRAND ON SOCIAL MEDIA

Similar to how social media can help you communicate well, it also plays a large role in building and managing your personal brand.

Keeping with the DECA theme from the preface, in my role as the Leadership Specialist for Wisconsin DECA there have been years I have been in charge of screening applicants running for State Office

– the small team of students chosen to lead the entire State. In this process, I had a team of people looking through the social media accounts of all the applicants. In several cases, students did not move forward in the application process because of their personal brand online.

Your personal brand is developed both in person and online, and social media plays a huge role.

Student leaders understand social media can be used both as a way to build friendships, interact socially online,[21] and as a career tool. In any case, your actions online have the capacity to further your ideal personal brand or set it back.

I'd recommend you take a moment to think about your ideal personal brand before posting anything online.

When you've established your ideal personal brand, post about things in alignment with the image you want to create for yourself – things depicting your passions and personality. Make sure all of your social media accounts, whether it is Facebook, Twitter, Instagram, Snapchat, TikTok, LinkedIn, or elsewhere are current and consistent to your brand.

Remember, your brand is made up of the thoughts, feelings, and emotions others have about you. Do your best to post content that is in line with the adjectives for which you determined you'd like to be known.

While social media can be a great tool, it can also be detrimental to your image if used in the wrong way. Take a moment right now on your phone or computer to Google yourself. What comes up? Are the results in alignment with your personal brand? Do you like what you see[22]?

Before we move on, there is one last point that needs to be made about personal branding on social media. It is an incredibly important one

---

[21] Hence the term, "Social media."

[22] Didn't find yourself? Nothing come up? That's okay. This just means someone with your same name has built a stronger personal brand online than you currently have.

so don't underestimate the value of the upcoming thoughts simply because they are at the end of the chapter.

*Think before posting about controversial topics.*

If you have certain political opinions but do not intend to go into politics (i.e. a political platform is not a part of your personal brand), you may want to refrain from posting things that polarize you politically – you never know where a future employer will stand on the issues you're posting about.

If you have strong thoughts or feelings on controversial topics – topics such as abortion or gun rights,[23] you are fully entitled to those thoughts and opinions – student leaders absolutely need to have opinions on important topics. Now more than ever young people from all walks of life need to find their *voices* and *engage* in the conversation.

My word of caution is not about holding back or withdrawing your voice. My simple word of caution is to think about your personal brand and what you would like to be known for before posting online. If you don't, you may end up down a wormhole of social media conversations you never meant to be a part of – and you'll wish you stuck closer to topics you are truly passionate about.

Social media can be an amazing tool for the personal brand of a student leader – it can support your career, help you network, and keep you engaged with current events.

From a career standpoint – if you want to be a sports journalist, create a new Twitter account and post about a team, player, or current events. This will help you gain credibility and is a great start.

From a networking standpoint – if you want to be a nurse, reach out on Linkedin[24] to nurse recruiters or nursing schools and ask questions about what they're looking for in future applicants.

---

[23] Both of which were extremely controversial when this was being written – hopefully the world has more clarity on these issues at the time you're reading it.

[24] LinkedIn is a resource to help you start networking. In fact, according to Forbes Magazine, 98% of recruiters and 85% of hiring managers use LinkedIn as a resource to hire new employees. Use this to your advantage. Add professional and personal contacts. Portray yourself as someone a company wants to hire and it might pay off.

From a current events standpoint – if you're interested in business, set up Google alerts for certain companies and track their activities. It will give you a lot to talk about in job interviews.

There are so many ways to advance your personal brand through social media. However, it is a double-edged sword. Be sure to spend as much time thinking about and protecting your personal brand online as you do expanding it.

## PERSONAL BRANDING IN ACTION

Young adult author John Green and his brother Hank created a YouTube channel in 2007 after the release of his first book, when he was still relatively unknown. He discussed anything and every-thing important to him, allowing his personality to shine through in a weekly video series called Brotherhood2.0. Since then, he has gained a huge following of loyal fans and launched events such as Project for Awesome and VidCon. He was recently listed as one of TIME's 100 most influential people. The ability to reach out to his fans through YouTube, Tumblr, Facebook, and Twitter has furthered his career and allowed him to gain visibility as an author and Internet personality.

• • •

By establishing your ideal personal brand, you're better able to work on *becoming* this brand. The more your actions reflect the adjectives you've outlined the more other people will begin to describe you this way.

While you can't always control how others view you, you can always choose *your actions*.

Clearly define what you want to be known for. When you do this, the next step is to do your best to *look* and *act* the part. People tend to believe what they consistently experience. The more your everyday actions align with the adjectives you chose for your ideal brand, the more you will start to see others naturally describing you in this way.

Always remember: your actions are constantly working to form the thoughts, feelings, and emotions others have about you.

Jaspreet became "The DECA Guy" because he consistently represented the organization as best he could. Creating and maintaining this personal brand for him has led to a career in the industry of his dreams and a lifetime of world travel.

Father John Naus became known as the caring, thoughtful man who brought smiles into the lives of so many.

Ben, our high school soccer captain, became known as the upperclassmen who brought people together to build a cohesive team on the field.

What could building an amazing personal brand mean for you?

Where might it lead you? What might you accomplish?

Your personal brand matters; *think* about what your ideal personal brand looks like, then take *action* every day to *become* it.

## CHAPTER 2 ACTION PACKED DISCUSSION QUESTIONS

1. *What are some positive words that describe your current brand?*

2. *What are some negative ones? How can you eliminate or work to change these?*

3. *Think of someone with positive social ascriptions[25]. How do they brand themselves?*

4. *How can you use your online presence to create or further a positive brand?*

---

[25] Do you know what this word means? Did you look it up? Start applying the lessons in this book today!

Chapter 3 Preface
# MORE THAN A GAME

When I was a junior in high school, our principal, Mr. Blankush, was diagnosed with ALS, also known as Lou Gehrig's Disease. This is a very serious and fatal disease – his diagnosis shocked our school and community.

Personally, I had several positive encounters with Mr. Blankush prior to his diagnosis. I knew he had been working to create a positive environment in our school, and the news hit me hard.

Knowing there would be hefty medical expenses associated with treating the disease, our community was ready to help, but how?

I sat down with Mr. Patterson, a teacher with whom I had spent a great deal of time throughout high school and talked with him about getting students involved in the effort to help raise funds for our principal. He was very open to ideas, and after crossing a few ideas off the brainstorm list, I said, "What about a student-faculty basketball game?"

Our eyes lit up at the idea. All of a sudden, more ideas started to fly, and a real plan started to come together.

"We could invite people from the community to watch. We could get local businesses to sponsor it."

He loved the idea and we got to work immediately to set a date and get people working on the details. It was a mad dash to put the event together.

We organized students to make phone calls to local businesses. We asked friends and family members to make fliers and put them up around town. It was a special task to recruit the right teachers to play in the game, and some of them even put together skits and asked if they could perform them during timeouts.

When the day of the event rolled around, Mr. Patterson and I weren't sure how it would all turn out. We crossed our fingers and hoped for a good turnout, as we only wanted the best for Mr. Blankush.

The event became a huge success. Hundreds of people from around the community came piling in to our high school gym. There were moments of hilarious fun from the teacher skits, and a hard-fought basketball game ensued.

There was a 50/50 raffle, concession stands, and in-game entertainment like a dance-off and a paper airplane toss competition.

My favorite part of the evening was watching Mr. Blankush in his wheelchair look on from the front row with a wide smile throughout the evening.

At the end of the event, Mr. Blankush had a moment at center court to express his gratitude for everyone who attended and the work that was put in. After he spoke, we were able to present him with a large check from the evening.

With just over a month of planning, our community was able to raise over $8,000 for Mr. Blankush's treatments.

I have thought about the event many times since then, and they are always warm memories.

At the end of the day, could we have made more money? Probably.

Would another event or idea have been just as successful? I'm sure.

But looking back, I've come to understand that the event didn't have to be perfect; the only thing that mattered was that *something was happening*.

Too often, students wait for the perfect time or the ideal situation to take action, and many times, this leads to no action at all.

In this scenario, our school and community recognized an opportunity in which we could make a difference, and we moved forward *quickly* to make something happen.

This is the reason no one today is talking about how we wished we had done more when Mr. Blankush got the news of this terrible disease; we talk about how cool it was to see a community rally in support of our principal.

Mr. Blankush passed away due to his battle with ALS, but not before feeling the support of an entire community coming together on his behalf.

He was always so grateful for the community that rallied around him throughout his time of struggle, and he will be remembered for his kindness and gratitude even in the midst of such an awful situation.

The student-faculty basketball game was held again the following year, and I was told they had higher attendance, raised more money, and had even more in-game "entertainment" than the first year.

When I graduated from high school, Mr. Patterson gave me a framed photo of all the students who participated in the game – and Mr. Blankush was smiling at the center.

At the bottom of the photo, he included a quote from John Wooden – a quote that brought tears to my eyes at the time and is still quite meaningful to me today:

> *"You can't live a full life without doing something for someone who will never be able to repay you."*

Taking initiative is the moment when positive *thought* becomes positive *action*.

This chapter is all about when, where, and how you can take initiative as a student leader.

In this chapter, I'll cover:

- When to step up and when to step back
- How to get started
- Outshining your peers
- The myth of well-roundedness
- Getting passionate

Chapter 3
# TAKING INITIATIVE

*"Don't wait for good things to happen to you. If you go out and make some good things happen, you will fill the world with hope, you will fill yourself with hope."*

—Barack Obama

Oftentimes, students want to get involved without the responsibility – they want to be a part of the action without doing any of the work.

A student leader recognizes the value of increased responsibility and chases down opportunities to become more involved.

Student leaders know that with more *responsibility* comes more *learning*, and with more *learning* comes more *success*.

In my experience traveling the country as a speaker, leadership trainer, and consultant, I can tell you with absolute certainty that not every student takes initiative – which is why it's such a valuable leadership quality that sets certain students apart.

Taking initiative means doing more than what is required.

It means recognizing opportunities to act, a willingness to see projects through, and being passionate about ways to improve the world.

Taking initiative helps young people gain credibility as leaders. *Credibility* is a personal brand characteristic that is obtained over time – it simply means people trust and believe in you.

Stepping up and taking action when action is required is a way for student leaders to gain credibility – it is a way for others to see and understand not just who you would like to be – but who you are *becoming*.

People will notice when you accept responsibility, even if it doesn't feel like it.

This chapter will get you ready to take initiative – to be a part of the *action* and step up in meaningful ways to challenges that arise.

## THAT'S MY CUE

How will you know when to take initiative and when to let others lead?[26]

As you gain experience (which comes from taking initiative), you will get better at recognizing moments that call for action. Until then, here are a few tips:

### Take Initiative!

» Being directly asked to fulfill a position of leadership is the clearest cue to take initiative. Whether you're chosen to be a captain or someone simply asks for some help on a project, take advantage – it means people think you're qualified to lead. I've personally noticed moments where others believe in a young person more than the young person believes in himself or herself – sometimes you have to trust that you are capable, even if you feel you are not, and believe the person who has asked you to lead has your best interests in mind.

---

[26] There are definitely moments when either can be appropriate.

» Sometimes you have to read between the lines. Verbal and nonverbal expressions of stress are cues to offer some assistance. If someone appears frustrated about a group project, you might say, "My time is a little limited this week, but is there a specific part I can help you with?" This way, you are not overcommitting, but you show your investment in the project and the individual.

» Announcements or fliers that call for leaders or volunteers are invitations to become involved. Look out for opportunities to make a difference in whatever capacity you can.

> YOU SAID IT!
>
> *"I like my voice to be heard, and if not me, then who? The biggest thing is leading by example."*
>
> —DANA AHMED
> FORMER ASB AND KEY CLUB PRESIDENT, KAMIAKIN HIGH SCHOOL

» If you notice a need for something, answer it. Just as the community rallied around Mr. Blankush when he received his diagnosis, student leaders are ready to spring into action when a moment calls for it. If your school has a demand for a club it doesn't already have, start one. If an organization could use a fundraising chair but doesn't have one, create the position. Act on your ideas to make improvements in your community and school.

» Finally, be sure to keep track of your *personal initiative*. This means that you can try to solve big problems, step up when asked, and always have your eyes on becoming a great leader – but if you're not treating people well along the way, none of it will matter. *Personal initiative* is about being nice. It is about building qualities that people gravitate towards – patience, generosity, kindness, etc. Treat those in positions under you as equals. Never flaunt your position or skills. Followers are quite often just as important as leaders as nothing great can be accomplished without a group of dedicated members working towards a common goal. Listen to others' input[27] and let them know you value their ideas and time. These are aspects of *personal initiative* that are just as vital as the big moments in the previous paragraph.

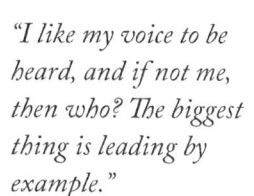

---

[27] Actually listen, don't just nod and smile.

## WHEN TO STEP BACK

It is not always advantageous to *step up*. In certain instances, even the best leaders recognize the opportunity to *step back*.

You'll notice that I used the word *opportunity* to describe stepping back and letting others lead. True leaders see it as a *privilege* to allow others to shine if it means the entire team can achieve greater success.

I also want to clarify – average students *step back* every day.

However, average students don't change the world. Average students step back because they are *afraid*. They are scared of what would happen if they stepped up so they choose to never take initiative.

Student leaders *step back* because they see an opportunity for someone else to lead. This is a good thing. Leaders recognize situations in which their own skills would better be used in a supporting role, and they get the right people in the right places.

The overall goal of a student leader is to facilitate the greatest amount of team success.

If stepping back can help achieve this goal, it is in a student leader's best interest to do so.

Below are some examples of times when it might be more advantageous to *step back* as opposed to *stepping up*.

- Freshmen on a soccer team typically do not walk into their first high school practice as leaders – they get there by recognizing opportunities and getting involved. Gaining credibility as a leader takes time. Move up on a sports team by working hard, actively expressing your enthusiasm, and respecting the coaches and leaders who were there before you – I could have probably done more of this with my high school basketball experience.
- When someone organizes a Student Council fundraiser – do not say, "This could be done better if I was in charge." A hostile takeover rarely works out.[28] It will force the people involved to

---
[28] Political dictators often learn this the hard way.

- pick sides, and in the end, will cause the entire fundraiser to fall apart. Offer your assistance and time, but let others lead. Being a follower can be a good thing – it lends you some perspective on how to lead well by watching someone else at the helm, and if, over time, the organization feels you would be a better leader, accept your move to leadership with dignity and grace.

- To piggy-back off the last example – if you are a Sophomore in band and a Senior is in first chair for your instrument, he or she should not be your enemy! Your job is to learn everything you can from people who are ahead of you. Take their strengths and apply them to your future leadership positions and notice their mistakes so you can avoid them when you become a leader. Ask the Senior how he/she got there, or how many hours a day he/she practices, or how to stand out in band – through this course of action, you'll most likely make a friend and ally even if you end up overtaking the Senior for first chair.[29]

- If you are in a leadership position, encourage others to get involved! It's the best way to increase enthusiasm about a project. This is how leaders can step back even if they are in charge. If you recognize another person may be able to carry out a piece of a project better than you, give them the chance to lead. For most young people, *pride* stands in the way of letting others have the credit. Great student leaders want success for their team and work toward the completion of a goal – in this ideal scenario, who gets the credit becomes less important.

## HOW TO GET GOING

In 2010, Facebook headquarters had painted on their wall this simple message:

***Done is better than perfect.***

*Not knowing where to start* is a common sentiment that prevents us from taking initiative.

---

[29] But don't be offended if the Senior doesn't take it very well. Some people are petty.

As a student leader, it is your goal to not get *trapped by inaction*.

If you don't know where to begin, ask someone. If you still don't know, write out a plan. If you still don't know, just start somewhere and make adjustments as you go.

**The worst thing you can do is nothing.**

As I mentioned in Chapter 1, sometimes you need to think:

*I just need to take one action.*

One action can facilitate new thoughts, new ideas, and be the start of a tremendous journey.

You have ideas – make them happen.

Your first attempt at anything won't be perfect, but don't let that stop you from taking the initiative.

I've always admired the learning capacity of children – a child learns much faster than an adult. One of the reasons for this is the child's ability to fail without judgment. When a child doesn't do something correctly, they typically don't say, "I'm just never going to be good at this so I might as well give up." But adults say things like this all the time!

A child understands they aren't going to be perfect at anything on the first try – which tends to take the pressure off – it gives them the ability to try something, learn from it, and try again.

Take a lesson from Facebook. Done is better than perfect. *A rough draft is better than no draft.* You can learn far more from chasing your ideas than you can by just thinking about them.

Remember my student-faculty basketball game?

I mentioned we could have most likely made more money with a different event or that we could have gotten more of the community involved – but when time isn't on your side,[30] doing *something* is far

---

[30] And it rarely is.

better than spending too much time *thinking* about the best option, and never doing *anything* at all.

Mark Zuckerberg, the Founder and CEO of Facebook, recognizes the value of running with his ideas, and attributes much of his success to it. In an open letter regarding Facebook's philosophy, he states:

> *Moving fast enables us to build more things and learn faster. However, as most companies grow, they slow down too much because they're more afraid of making mistakes than they are of losing opportunities by moving too slowly. We have a saying: "Move fast and break things." The idea is that if you never break anything, you're probably not moving fast enough.*

You don't have to recklessly start taking action – sometimes the proper way to take initiative is to *seek advice*.

Seeking proper advice is an *action*, and it can be incredibly helpful.

If you are the captain of the basketball team and you think the team should start using a full-court press, it's foolish to start doing it in games without your coach knowing.

If you are on the prom planning committee and you think there should be more streamers hung from the ceiling, it's not recommended[31] that you try to hang them before consulting your teacher or advisor.

Taking initiative can be calculated, but it shouldn't be slow.

It should be opportunistic, but not stupid.

By all means, dive in – just avoid diving into the rocks.

## INITIATIVE SETS YOU APART – IN A GOOD WAY

In school, people who seem to "care too much" sometimes get stuck with the unfair title of suck-ups.

---

[31] AKA potentially really dangerous

There is nothing I hate more.[32]

In the corporate world, people who care are *assets*. They are beneficial to the company for which they work.

Somehow, our culture instills in young people that if they care too much about something, they become uncool.

I want you to forget this outdated thinking *immediately*.

*Passion* and *initiative* are valuable – they add value to your school, community, resume, and self. Embrace your passions and take initiative even if, during high school, people don't always understand you[33].

People will begin to understand when you *step up* in moments that call for it. You'll begin to earn respect from teachers, future employers, and over time even your peers. Everyone wants someone who goes the extra mile to be on his or her side.

On a college application or in an interview, you can reference specific organizations or projects in which you took initiative.

> **YOU SAID IT!**
>
> "Student leaders aren't always the most respected people. Other students might criticize the dance you put on or the event you organized. But student leaders are trying to serve others. That's our goal. We're doing it to help other people and that mindset is so important. If you're doing it for the wrong reasons you won't get nearly as much out of it."
>
> – MORGAN RAJALA, FORMER CASL (CALIFORNIA ASSOCIATION OF STUDENT LEADERS) PRESIDENT

Hard work, leadership, and teamwork are valuable skill sets, and are all byproducts of *stepping up* and *getting involved*. These skills will set you apart from others who may lack your initiative and not get involved like you do.

---

[32] Well, there are probably things I hate more, but you know what I mean.

[33] Author John Green has this to say about being nerdy: "Nerds like us are allowed to be enthusiastic about stuff. Nerds are allowed to love stuff, like jump-up-and-down-in-the-chair-can't-control-yourself love it. When people call people nerds, mostly what they're saying is 'you like stuff.' Which is just not a good insult at all."

As you take initiative you will gain *credibility* as a leader which will help people believe in you and your goals.

So, bring on any nickname from someone who doesn't understand your passion, drive, and initiative. "Suck-up," "Do-gooder," "Overachiever…" and whatever else the kids are saying.

Don't let the world around you tell you that you can't be enthusiastic about something, or care about something, or try hard at something – look right back at them and tell them they SHOULD do more of all of those things. There are young people at every school around the country who lack the ability to care, and nothing is scarier to me; these students have low levels of empathy and are often indifferent to the struggles of others. And not so surprisingly, these are the young people judging leaders for stepping up; I don't know about you, but I'm cheering for the young people who care.

Don't let the fear of being judged keep you from accepting new and different responsibilities.

Be confident in your abilities to take initiative and step up. Take a risk, try that new and out-of-the-box idea, join that club or organization – it might pay off in a big way.

At the end of the day, when you get recognized and rewarded for always rising to challenges, stepping up when others don't, and taking initiative, no one will be judging you. You will only be applauded for bringing new ideas and executing them well.

And if people do judge you, who cares? You'll feel so fulfilled because you filled your cup from the bottom, you'll know you're moving towards the best version of yourself, and you'll be taking initiative in line with what you care about. I can promise you these will be more meaningful in the long run than whatever anyone else may think now.

## THE MYTH OF WELL-ROUNDEDNESS

Oh no.

The downside of taking initiative…

There is an overwhelming pressure among students to have *enough* leadership positions.

Isn't that a crux of a word? *Enough.*

It's hard to ever have enough – enough money, enough experience, enough friends, enough followers.

Before continuing, I'd like to take this moment to tell you that you *are enough*. Right now, exactly how you are today.

This book is meant to make you the *best version of you*. It is definitely not meant to turn you into anyone else. You are you for a reason.

I firmly believe you have enormous value, and that your uniqueness is something no one else can bring to this world. I'm glad you're here.

Even though we've never met, I can promise you that *you are enough*, and I hope you believe me.

Back to leadership.

Students tend to overload themselves in order to appear well-rounded on increasingly competitive college applications. They take every AP class, sign up for every organization, play every sport, and usually forget how to sleep along the way.

Involvement is great, and so is the responsibility that comes with it. Taking initiative can teach us so much about ourselves and others, and allow us to grow as leaders. But indiscriminately joining organizations for the sake of adding it to your resume is unrewarding. You'll feel unfulfilled, you'll accomplish less in each organization, and *you'll burn yourself out before you even finish high school.*

Real student leaders become involved in what they're passionate about and remove the clubs, organizations, and sports that don't fit.

The added responsibility of a leadership position should be challenging, but fulfilling. It should be something you *care* about deep down.

If you're one of these young people, you may also be interested in hearing that most colleges actually want to see the *depth* of your involvement, not the *width*. This means, they want to see how much you were able to *accomplish* in the organizations you chose to be a part of rather than simply judging you based on the number of organizations on your resume.

You'll have more success digging a well a mile deep and an inch wide, than a mile wide and an inch deep.

Taking on too much can become a burden and add unneeded stress to your life. Focus on your passions and make a real impact on the organizations you choose to be in.

Don't spread yourself so thin that you can't give projects you truly care about the attention they deserve. Your involvement should go deep, and not necessarily wide. Being well rounded is overrated – your edges are where your strengths are. Employers more often look for someone passionate and talented in one area, than mediocre in many. What do you care about – art? Fitness? Politics? Get involved. If there isn't an organization that fits your interests, start your own. Focus on your strengths and what comes most naturally to you, and take initiative in developing it.

## YOU SAID IT!

*"A lot of kids in high school, including me, joined clubs they hated but felt obligated to join so that they could add it to their list of involvement and leadership skills. But by my junior year, I realized I didn't care about half of the clubs I was in, and became less and less motivated to stay involved. I felt like I was wasting my time, and my participation waned. That's when I decided to try something different. I joined some new clubs that I actually cared about – Relay for Life Committee, Empowering Women Club, started Bicycling Club with my friends, and became more involved in athletics and eventually was captain of two sports. Getting into leadership positions in a few organizations I actually loved was much more rewarding than membership in many."*

—KAYLA SPENCER
FORMER MARQUETTE UNIVERSITY TRACK & FIELD STUDENT ATHLETE

## GET PASSIONATE

No matter your passion, it is much easier to take *action* on something you truly care about. If you love computers, try to get involved in clubs where you can use your skills; if you love photography, buy a camera (or borrow one from your school) and start taking pictures. You can even submit your photos for the yearbook if you want more people to see them.

The important part is that you start.

You'll be amazed at how easy it is to put time and effort into something when you're truly passionate about it. Take a moment to write down a few things you love to do – are there any opportunities you may be missing to apply your expertise?

You don't need to be "well-rounded" to make a lasting impact.

As a student leader, it is important to know when to *step up*. There is something to be said about "Doers;" those people who just get things done. We all know people like this – at times I've wondered how these people do it all.

Then I heard something I'll never forget – "If you want to get something done, ask a busy person."

The people who take initiative are the ones who learn how to do stuff.[34] The ones who are continuously planning, organizing, and just *trying* are the ones who start to stand out from the crowd.

It is not impossible to be this person.

Use the tips from this chapter to take initiative in the areas in which you are passionate. It will set you apart as a student leader.

---

[34] I was once told never to use the word "stuff" in my writing so I've made it a point to include the word "stuff" at least once in all of my books. It feels more real to me.

# **CHAPTER 3** ACTION PACKED DISCUSSION QUESTIONS

*1. List a few broad areas that interest you (ex. sports, band, photography, etc.).*

_____

_____

_____

*2. How can you take initiative in these areas? Are there organizations you could get involved with, or does the position need to be created?*

_____

_____

_____

*3. How can you "move fast and break things" in regards to your projects and involvement?*

_____

_____

_____

*4. What are one or two areas of your life in which you should probably take a step back?*

_____

_____

_____

Chapter 4 Preface
# FLORIDA OR BUST

In doing the research for this book, I talked with two high school students from Wisconsin named Hannah and Grace who, like Jaspreet, were involved in an organization called DECA at the time of our conversation.[35]

They described to me a project they had been working on for their DECA competition. The project had become a large part of their day-to-day lives simply because of the amount of work they needed to accomplish - they had been working on it for 7 months, and had 2 months left to finish.

The project involved choosing a local business to study, finding an age group the business is not serving well, and offering suggestions to reach the underserved market.

They told me about the ins-and-outs of the project – how they had decided on an RV business that was neglecting the younger market because young people most likely do not have the expendable income to purchase an RV. They told me about their goals and how they managed their time. They told me about the presentation they were

---

[35] Don't worry, plenty of other organizations are represented later in the book.

preparing to "wow" the business at the end of the 9 months (and the judges in the DECA competition).

As they were enthusiastically explaining every piece of the project to me, something occurred to me. They had been working on this project for 7 months and they were still excited about it!

How many times have you been working on a project for 7 minutes and realized you'd rather be doing something else?[36]

After 7 months, they had 2 months left to finish the project. I'm sure I'm not the only one who thinks 9 months is a long time to focus on one project.[37]

Homework assignments usually last an hour or two, the longer ones could be a week or two. 9 months? That's a long time.

I asked Grace and Hannah how they scheduled their time to make sure everything came together.

They told me that they started with their end goal in mind: they wanted their project to get them to the International DECA competition in Orlando, Florida.

To do this, they would need their names to be called at the State DECA competition in Wisconsin.

With the vision set, they worked to set weekly goals.

"We are really busy with work and other activities so we set weekly goals for ourselves. We knew that if we didn't do that we wouldn't get it done in a timely manner," Hannah told me.

It seemed to me that they had it all figured out, but successful projects don't always come without a road bump or two.

"About a month ago, we thought we were pretty much done with our project. Our teacher looked at it and said, 'You guys are nowhere near

---

[36] You are definitely not alone if this is you.

[37] Unless that project is creating another human – then 9 months is the perfect amount of time.

being done.' It was frustrating to hear. We had to go back and look at it and understand that his feedback was important. If you don't listen to the feedback it doesn't help you."

The work they put into their project was impressive and the way they managed their time and dealt with feedback is commendable.

They finished their project on time and were happy with how their presentations went.

Then for the moment they were waiting for – would they make it to the International DECA competition?

They waited nervously at the State awards ceremony to hear if their names would be called.[38]

When the moment of truth came, their hard work paid off.

The announcer read their names, and their entire DECA chapter jumped out of their chairs and cheered for them as they made their way to the stage.

They received medals and a trophy and wore smiles on the stage that could be seen from the back of the room.

The 9 months they had spent putting together a project they could be proud of helped them reach their end goal – they had made it to the International competition in Florida.

Student leaders, like Hannah and Grace, learn to manage projects.

Projects can be big or small. They can last for 9 months or 9 minutes. They can be anything from organizing the best prom ever while in Student Council or prepping to show animals at the fair as a member of 4-H.

Like communication, personal branding, and taking initiative there are ways student leaders think differently about the projects they take on.

---

[38] As it turned out, I was in attendance at the State event as well – after talking with them so much about their project, I was secretly nervous too.

In this chapter, you'll find everything you need to become a project management master. I'll talk about:

- Committing to a project (thinking differently)
- Setting SMART goals
- The benefits of delegation

Chapter 4
# PROJECT MANAGEMENT

*"No one can whistle a symphony. It takes a whole orchestra."*

—H.E. Luccock

Project management isn't simply about homework and clubs. For the sake of clarity, when I talk about a project I simply mean anything that takes effort and organization to complete. I bet you can think of plenty of things in your life that fit this description.

However, this chapter is just as much about *mindset* as it is about the actual projects and work.

How we choose to see our work quite often is a predictor of the quality of work we produce.

When we look at our projects and work with a *positive mindset*, we are much more capable of delivering successful outcomes. Remember how excited Grace and Hannah were even after 7 months of work on their project? When we are *happy* we have the opportunity to do our work, we tend to see *better results*.

In his book, The Happiness Advantage, Shawn Achor explains how society typically looks at happiness:

"When I achieve success, then I'll be happy."

Yet, all of his research suggests the inverse is more relevant:

"When I'm happy, I'll achieve more success."

Don't believe your mindset can have an impact on your ability to manage projects effectively? Below is an excerpt from The Happiness Advantage that may change your mind:

"In the Introduction, I mentioned the impressive meta-analysis of happiness research that brought together the results of over 200 scientific studies on nearly 275,000 people – and found that happiness leads to success in nearly every domain of our lives, including marriage, health, friendship, community involvement, creativity, and, in particular, our jobs, careers, and businesses. Data abounds showing that happy workers have higher levels of productivity, produce higher sales, perform better in leadership positions, and receive higher performance ratings and higher pay. They also enjoy more job security and are less likely to take sick days, to quit, or to become burned out."

Unsurprisingly, the way you *think* about the projects you work on will change the way you *manage* them. With this in mind, we'll first dive in to the *mindset* of a successful young project manager, then we'll discuss the x's and o's of taking a project from start to finish.

## THE COMMITTED MIND

You learned in the last chapter when to *step up* and when to *step back* – if you are applying this lesson well, the projects you take on should be ones to which you can fully commit and make a *real impact*.

In this way, project management becomes less of a burden and more of an enjoyable experience.

Any project will require commitment – both mentally and physically.

A *committed mind* makes the mental decision to approach a project with enthusiasm before the project even begins.

If you're keeping track, the formula so far is:

- Fill your cup from the bottom – *become* the right person
- Enhance *who* you are and determine how you'd like to be *perceived*
- Learn to *step up* or *step back*
- Approach your work with a *committed mind*

The student leader with a *committed mind* doesn't quit when something doesn't go perfectly – they have made the decision to stick it out until the project or goal is complete.

Only after you have given *intentional thought* to a project should you begin to work on it.

You may be thinking, "I can't always decide what projects I have to work on."

Totally makes sense.

If the "project" is simply a homework assignment, you probably didn't have any say in whether you had to complete it or not.

However, your mindset still matters. For moments like these, take 30 seconds to mentally commit to finishing it in one sitting without looking at your phone. Something as simple as this will drastically decrease how long it takes you to complete the assignment.

If the "project" is organizing a pep rally for your school, mentally commit to working on it all the way up until the date when it happens[39] – with this mentality, you'll assure yourself, your teachers, and your peers that they can count on you to manage the project as well as you can and not give up or not do your part when it gets difficult.

A *committed mind* has the ability to change a homework assignment into an interesting challenge. It has the ability to change exhaustion

---

[39] And maybe commit to cleaning up the day after if it is happening in the evening.

into determination. It has the ability to keep you focused even when those around you slow down or want to quit.

One simple shift in *mindset* can make an enormous impact on your outcomes.

When it comes to the physical nature of project management, it is important to consider whether you are willing to put time and energy into a project before you say, "Yes" to taking it on.

It may be a good idea to evaluate the responsibilities of a leadership position before you accept the role.

If you feel uncertain about a project, seek council from another student or an adult you trust before moving forward. Ask questions about time commitment or expectations.

Keep in mind, this person may give advice you still do not agree with – it is okay to go against the advice you receive. However, this doesn't mean you shouldn't get advice in the first place. With more *perspective* you gain more *wisdom* and will feel more capable of making an *informed decision* about your involvement.

If the project doesn't align with your personal brand or you can't commit to the time and energy necessary to do a great job, pass on the position and channel your involvement elsewhere.

If the project in question is for school or a grade, you may not have much of a choice as to whether you complete it, however, you still have a choice when it comes to your mindset.

Committing to a project is not about simply having *complete control* of which projects you take on, it is about switching your focus to what you *can control* – your mindset – to create the best possible outcome you can.

As a general rule of thumb, don't say yes to a project if you have too much on your plate. Only take on as much as you can handle.[40]

---

[40] Or maybe just a little more – most people can handle more than they think.

Once you commit, you have a responsibility to see the project through to its completion.

What projects do you currently have on your plate? Are you looking at these projects with a positive mindset? Are you fully committed to these projects?

If your answers to the questions above are unfavorable, you may need a change of mindset, a change of project, or a change of both.

## ACTUALLY SETTING GOALS

Most students have had goal-setting techniques preached to them more times than they care to remember.

There is a reason for this: *most students still don't set them!*

I've mentioned this book is about bringing *positive thought* into *positive action* – this is where your actions begin to matter.

Imagine for a moment you are playing in the State Championship basketball game. Your team is down by one and you have the ball in your hands. You drive to the basket, and just as the clock is about to expire, you get fouled and sent to the free throw line. You have two shots – make them both and your team wins. Make one and you go to overtime. Miss them both and your team loses the biggest game of the year.

> QUOTABLE:
> 
> *"A goal is a dream with a deadline."*
> 
> —NAPOLEON HILL

Luckily for you, you're the star of the team and making free throws is something you can do in your sleep.

Now imagine you are in this same situation, but you've never shot a basketball before (disregard the fact that it would have been a terrible decision for the coach to give you the ball at the end of a close game).

How would you feel stepping to the free throw line of the biggest game of the year knowing you have absolutely no idea how to shoot?

This is what trying to accomplish tasks without setting goals is like.[41]

Personally, as someone who loves basketball, thinking about this situation makes my palms a little sweaty – it gives me anxiety to think about being at the free throw line without the tools necessary to succeed.

It should give you similar anxiety thinking about managing a project in your life without setting any goals or creating an agreed upon vision. These are the tools necessary to succeed – it would be foolish to jump ahead without taking a moment to set the foundation for success.

Student leaders understand the value of setting goals. They know setting goals around the projects they have mentally and physically committed to will help them reach higher levels of success.

Simply *knowing* how to set goals and never *creating* them is not helpful.

I'll say this again in case you're listening to the audio version of this book and need it emphasized.

Simply *knowing* how to set goals and never *creating* them is not helpful.

Here are a few techniques that really make a difference when forming goals:

### The Big Picture

Before beginning a project, look at it from a distance. What needs to be accomplished? What is the purpose of your effort? It is easy to get caught up on the little details of a project. Taking a step back will help you focus on the project as a whole. You'll have time to get more specific, but it is always helpful to know the direction you are headed before diving in.

### Write Them Down

Research done by Dr. Gail Matthews of Dominican University of California states that written goals have a 33% greater chance

---

[41] I could have taken this analogy a lot of different directions – I felt like this was the least cliché of my options.

of being realized than those that stay in your head. Getting your goal on paper holds you accountable. You'll be more motivated to take the necessary steps with the end goal constantly in mind.

> **PRO TIP #4**
>
> Write your goals on your mirror or post them on your bulletin board – somewhere you will see them every day. This will force you to keep your goal in mind and off the back burner, even when life gets in the way.

### Tell Someone

When you share your goals with a friend they will hold you accountable[42] – especially if they are invested in the project as well. If you tell your friend you want to start running 10 miles per week, you won't want to go back on your word. Knowing someone expects you to complete your goal can give you motivation. Ask them to cheer you on if you start slacking. It helps when you have someone to give you a little push every now and then.

## SMART GOALS, SMARTER STUDENTS

Don't be dumb. Make your goals SMART (I would never call you dumb unless I was making a corny joke about SMART goals).

Average students all over the world have "goals." However, without any structure these "goals" do not help them achieve anything beyond ordinary.

While running leadership camps in Oklahoma several years ago, I ran 8 sessions on goal setting with hundreds of middle school students over the course of 4 weeks. At the start of each session, I asked everyone to write out a goal and share it with someone near them.

I can't tell you how many goals I heard like these:

"Get better at doing homework."

---

[42] This is typically called an "Accountability Partner."

"Run faster in track this year."

"Have a better relationship with my brother."

While each of these are great *thoughts*, they miss the pivotal elements necessary to successfully bring *thought* to *action*.[43]

Student leaders know setting goals is not child's play. Creating a proper vision and defining it well drastically increases our ability to achieve higher levels of success.

The SMART goal framework is a handy acronym that can easily be worked through by anyone – there are small variations of the acronym depending on the person delivering the information. The elements of the acronym I like best are:

- Specific
- Measurable
- Attainable
- Reaching
- Timely

Follow this framework to make goals like a student leader.

### Specific

It's impossible to quantify your progress if specific goals are not established. Utilize *numbers* and *names*. *Numbers* give everyone involved a tangible picture of what success is and allows you to track your progress (ex. $2,000 raised during a fundraiser). *Names* can be used to keep others accountable (ex. John is responsible for posters for the fundraiser). If people are not assigned to specific tasks, everyone will assume someone else is doing it, and it won't get done. Other items to be specific about would be dates/

> **QUOTABLE:**
>
> *"If everyone is responsible, then no one is responsible."*
>
> — ROBIN SHARMA

---

[43] Which is the entire goal of this book.

deadlines, benchmarks (checkpoints along the way), and work that needs to be done to reach the end-goal.

### Measurable

It's easy to fall into the trap of setting a goal around something immeasurable. Vague goals like, "Have a successful bake sale" are ineffective as there is no mention of how success will be measured. A better goal may be to generate $500 in sales by creating posters, posting on social media, and writing to a local newspaper. This goal is measurable because the outcome is defined by a specific dollar amount. A dollar amount is easy to measure, but how do you measure something like involvement? Make sure you don't say, "Get more people involved." Make your goal measurable by saying, "Get 25 people to attend the first meeting." As you may have noticed, measurement is all about *numbers* that can be *tracked*. If you can't track it, you can't measure it – be careful with this as it relates to social media measurement. You'll want to have specific ways to *track* engagement (followers, likes, shares, etc.) if your goal involves building or improving a social media presence.

### Attainable

Aiming high is one characteristic that serves student leaders well. While this is normally a positive trait, students can also get overbooked and stressed, and because of this over-commitment, feel disappointed with an outcome. When setting a goal, take a moment to look at what can realistically be accomplished. At times, this may take the help of a teacher or advisor. Earning $30,000 at a school bake sale is not realistic,[44] but earning $500 or $1,000 might be. It's a good idea to run your thoughts by others to ensure your goals are attainable.

### Reaching

Some experts will say "Realistic" when explaining the "R." In my mind, realistic is the same as attainable. While goals should be

---

[44] If you do accomplish this feat, please let me know. You must be selling some really good cupcakes, and I would like one (or ten).

attainable, they should also be *challenging*. This is where the word "Reaching" comes in. It comes back to student leaders' natural tendency to push themselves. No sense of fulfillment comes from easy goals. Using the bake sale example from earlier, no one would be impressed if the goal was to sell 3 items. Is it specific? Yes. Can you measure it? Yes. Is it attainable? Definitely. But you could buy 3 bake sale items by yourself and call it a day. This won't feel very fulfilling to anyone involved. Don't hesitate to reach a little when it comes to setting goals. Shooting for things that are just a little out of reach is a good thing – it will make achieving the goal much more meaningful for you and your team. Even if you do not reach your goal, you'll hopefully end up ahead of where you otherwise would have been. Note: you may want to set reaching goals privately with the team you're working with and keep them from the public. This may allow you to show success in the public eye even if you didn't make it all the way to your reaching goal privately.

**Timely**

Deadlines are your friend. Set a final deadline, and set up checkpoints along the way to ensure that progress is being made. Send reminders, set up meetings, and check in often to monitor progress. This will prevent everyone from cramming all of the work in at the last minute. Work to avoid this scenario at all times. Rush work is far less effective than work done on a specified timeline.

## YOU SAID IT!

*"I run track competitively. When I have an opportunity to race, I sometimes make goals for myself that I know are just a little ridiculous. This year, I decided I wanted to drop eight seconds from my personal best mile time. I knew I could drop time, but an eight-second drop was definitely a reach. I trained hard all season, and by the end of the year I dropped five and a half seconds. It's not what I set out to do, but I ran much faster than I would have if I hadn't given myself such a "scary" goal."*

—KAYLA SPENCER
FORMER MARQUETTE UNIVERSITY TRACK & FIELD STUDENT ATHLETE

## LONG TERM VS. SHORT TERM

You should have both long-term goals and short-term goals. Long-term goals make you think about the big picture and should be established first. Think of them as a final product – the big things you want to accomplish. Work backwards from your long-term goals to create smaller goals to be achieved along the way. They should be small steps that lead you to your long-term goal.

## DELEGATE

Many students manage projects on their own; student leaders inspire others to help them.

*Delegation* is the act of assigning sections of a goal to specific people.

To ensure deadlines are being met and expectations are being exceeded, effective student leaders allow others to take ownership.

Todd Gehrmann, founder and CEO of the leadership development company FOCUS Training, believes, "People support what they help to create." When members of a group feel they have been given ownership, they will be much more likely to invest time and energy to make it work.

When you are feeling overwhelmed or have taken on too many projects at once, don't be afraid to lend a teammate some of the responsibility. There's no shame in asking for help. You don't have to do everything on your own.

When I was in high school, I found it difficult to ask for help. I've now met hundreds of high school students who feel the same way. Asking for help is not easy – it makes us feel vulnerable. *What if they say no? What if they don't like my ideas? What if I can't count on the people I thought I could trust?*

My biggest piece of advice when it comes to asking for help is this:

PRACTICE.

Start small. Ask friends for something. Ask a teacher for assistance. Ask anyone anything.

What you are really doing when you practice asking for things is giving yourself permission to be *vulnerable*.

At the end of the day, the ability to embrace vulnerability in pursuit of a larger purpose can only be helpful.

I learned the value of *practice* during my first internship while I was a sophomore in college. I sat at a desk for 4 hours at a time and made cold-calls, trying to book longer meetings at a later date. Most people didn't pick up, some did and said no, and then every now and again I'd get what I was asking for; someone would say, "Yes." This taught me how to not take a "No" personally, and that over time, persistence pays off, practice makes (almost) perfect, and people are bound to eventually say "Yes."

As a student *leader*, you should be doing just that: *leading*.

Leading means you are not doing everything on your own.

It means you'll be much more effective by learning to delegate tasks and working well with others to accomplish your goal.

---

*"I've had to step up to the plate and take charge at home and in school, as I'm sure you have or will as well. When projects were assigned, I have always felt as if I were the leader in the group. Instead of doing all the work myself, or having other people do it, I have everyone work together to get the task done by delegation. When we work together not only does the job get done faster, but everyone can feel proud to have a part in the task at hand. When delegating tasks, it's important to not only divide up the work equally, but also to listen to the ideas of the group members. When the whole group has a say in the work, they all feel more obliged to do their part."*

—Makayla Gilbert
**Former Oregon FCCLA Vice President of Peer Education**

---

Learning to effectively set goals and manage projects will keep you on track to accomplishing all that you'd like to, and giving others an opportunity to help makes a huge difference.

Student leaders know that taking initiative is important, but unless that initiative is sustained over time and managed properly, the project will not get completed.

Take initiative as a student leader, then set goals and manage projects accordingly. When you start early and practice often, you will only improve in these areas over time.

## CHAPTER 4 ACTION PACKED DISCUSSION QUESTIONS

*1. What's one short-term project you have? How does it contribute to a longer-term goal? (Ex. short-term practice→every day. Long-term→win the competition)*

*2. Does your project have all of the elements of a SMART goal?*

*3. How can you get others more involved and invested in your goals?*

Chapter 5 Preface

# I JUST WANT A CHEESEBURGER

Gary Vaynerchuk has over a million followers on Twitter. He's pretty famous. He has been a judge at the Miss America Pageant and has founded several large companies. He has been one of my favorite entrepreneurs for a long time, and when I was a junior in college, I got the chance to meet him.

But I need to back this story up a bit.

Because the story is not about meeting Gary Vaynerchuk, though it was very cool; this story is about networking.

The way I got the opportunity to meet Gary V started with one simple act of defiance:

I refused to wait for a cheeseburger.

It sounds far-fetched, but let me explain.

A new restaurant had opened in Milwaukee called AJ Bombers. I had heard several things about it that sounded awesome. People were claiming they had the best cheeseburgers in town and they had a really great (and funny) social media presence. It sounded like a place I would enjoy. One Saturday, I got a small group of friends together to try AJ Bombers, but what we were told when we got there was disheartening.

"I'm sorry, sir. We have about a two-hour wait at the moment."

Bummer.

My friends and I left.

A few days later, we decided to try again. Different day – same result.

"I'm sorry, sir. We have about an hour-and-a-half wait at the moment."

Dang.

We left again.

At this point I was not very happy about being turned away not once, but twice by AJ Bombers – so I did the natural thing so many people do: I voiced my dissatisfaction on Twitter.[45]

I'm a pretty polite Twitter user, but I did let them know I would not be coming back anytime soon.

AJ Bombers responded immediately.

First, they invited me back. I told them I didn't have time and had already tried twice.

Then, they insisted I needed to try one of their burgers. I told them I just couldn't make the trip a third time.

Then, they offered to deliver me a burger on my college campus. I tried to work with them to find a time that fit my schedule and theirs, and in the end, nothing really seemed to work out.

This Twitter conversation lasted for weeks, and during this time I had been reading Gary Vaynerchuk's second book, The Thank You Economy. Just as I was thinking I was never giving AJ Bombers another chance, I stumbled upon a chapter in Gary's book that made me stop in my tracks.

---

[45] I'm sorry. I'm human.

The entire chapter was about AJ Bombers!

He talked about how this Milwaukee restaurant was crushing it – from their online marketing efforts to their effective use of social media – both things I was learning about in my college business classes.

This was my tipping point.

If my favorite entrepreneur was a fan of AJ Bombers, I needed to give it another chance.

So I tweeted to AJ Bombers asking when I should come in. We worked out a date and a time, and I prepped myself to wait in the long line that was sure to greet me as I entered the restaurant.

On the contrary, when I got to AJ Bombers, I was greeted with a large smile as soon as I walked in.

"Kyle? Hi, I'm Joe, I'm the owner of AJ Bombers. We have your table all set up."

Joe led us to the table, explained the menu, and said, "Also, anything you get today is completely on me. Get whatever you'd like; I'll cover it. I'm sorry we couldn't get you in here sooner."

I was surprised by the gesture, "Wow. Thanks so much, Joe."

He then asked, "Just out of curiosity, what changed your mind about coming in?"

I went on a long tangent about Gary Vaynerchuk - how he was my favorite entrepreneur and how his chapter on AJ Bombers ultimately got me to come back.

Joe smiled and said, "You know, he'll be in Milwaukee next week speaking at an exclusive event for presidents and vice presidents of companies in town."

I said, "Oh, really? That's pretty cool."

Then he said the words that blew my mind:

"Why don't you come to his event?"

The answer seemed obvious to me at first. I laughed and said, "Well I'm not a president or vice president of a company. I don't think I'm invited."

Joe just smiled and said, "Don't worry about it. I'll get you a ticket."

Through one Twitter conversation with a restaurant, I went from refusing to wait for a cheeseburger to meeting the owner of AJ Bombers – who turned out to be one of the most generous people I've ever met – to meeting my favorite entrepreneur, Gary Vaynerchuk.

What a 180! My experience went from vowing to never eat at AJ Bombers again to having Gary V personally sign my copy of his book.

I mentioned this story was about networking, and it is.

I had no idea the value a single tweet would bring me.

I didn't know I would meet Joe, and I definitely didn't know Joe would help me meet Gary.

Sometimes you simply don't know the effect others can have on your life. This is why networking – genuinely and without expectation – is so important.

Joe, however, knew exactly what he was doing.

He is a master networker, and it shows in the success of everything he does and every restaurant he opens.

His networking skills and extreme generosity have helped him open several more restaurants in multiple cities (including many more AJ Bombers locations – at the time of this writing, he even has an AJ Bombers location at the stadium of the Milwaukee Brewers).

With the extreme hospitality Joe showed me, I became a huge advocate and loyal customer of AJ Bombers. I have told this story about a thousand times, and encourage others often to eat at Joe's restaurants.

Joe brought extreme value to me, and I have been doing my best to return the favor ever since. This is the value of networking.

In this chapter I'll cover:

- How networking can affect your career, well-being, grades, and give you an overall edge
- Ultra-inclusivity
- *How* to go outside your comfort zone
- The art of the follow up
- Avoiding networking faux pas
- Making a strong first impression

Chapter 5
# NETWORKING

*"Networking is far more like 'farming' than it is 'hunting'. It's about cultivating relationships."*

—Dr. Ivan Misner[46]

Networking involves developing relationships with people for mutual benefit in your career or personal life.

It is *not* using others for your personal gain. It is *not* about schmoozing or being disingenuous so you can get in the social spotlight.

Networking *is* about asking, "How can I help?" not "What can I get?" It's about expanding your sphere of influence, serving others, and cultivating relationships. Just like with personal branding, networking involves marketing yourself, your beliefs, and your uniqueness. Developing mutually beneficial relationships can really come in handy – and it doesn't hurt to start early.

---

[46] The "Father of Networking", Ivan Misner is the founder of business networking organization BNI. He's also written sixteen books on the subject.

In my experience as well as talking to students around the country, networking can seem a little intimidating, which is a totally understandable and relatable feeling. The idea of developing a relationship with someone out of thin air, and hoping someday the thin-air relationships you've built will work in your favor as well as in favor of those with whom you've connected? Sounds like a lot to hope for.

However, I'd like to remove the overwhelming piece of the equation with one simple reminder:

You already do it.

Every day, you cultivate relationships with your friends, family, teammates, and classmates. You are constantly encountering new faces and adding and subtracting from your social circles. Networking isn't this far-fetched idea only professionals do – it is happening all around you every day.

Obviously, not every one of your relationships has the same purpose or level of intimacy – and that's okay. It's good to have relationships with different groups for different reasons. No one would expect you to love your volleyball coach like you love your father or mother.[47]

Networking is simply *interacting with purpose*.

Here's how networking can help you:

## CAREER

70% of all jobs are found through networking (US Bureau of Labor Statistics). People would rather hire someone they know to be trustworthy than a stranger they spent an hour interviewing. There may not even be a position available at the time of an interview (as you may recall from my experience with Kris and Matt and our fruit-shaped soap conversation in Chapter One), but because networking is a long-term process, when opportunities present themselves, you will

---

[47] Although, sometimes coaches and teachers do end up becoming more like family as young people spend more time with them.

have already established a connection and may even be first on their list. You may not even want a position at the company at the moment, but if an opportunity of interest comes up, you have an e-mail address and phone number to reach out later on.

**PRO TIP #5**

Along with networking in person, you can also connect with people through LinkedIn. Reach out to leaders in the profession you would like to pursue – it doesn't hurt to try.

## WELL-BEING

It's good to have different levels of relationships with people – you have your family, close friends, acquaintances, and peers. Networking allows us to find the people who truly build us up, personally and professionally. Student leaders strive to find the people who are positive forces in their lives.

## YOUR EDGE

Alexander Kjerulf, international speaker and author, believes that if you cannot "relate to your coworkers as human beings and build positive relationships, your career will suffer. Socializing and getting to know them as people will help you to communicate better, trust each other more, and work better together." You'll also be happier at work (or in a class, club, or sport) if you have positive people around you. Your ability to connect with those around you in any setting can influence your trajectory. There's a reason so many business deals get done on golf courses – the comfortable setting allows professionals to get to know each other on a personal level, leading to a higher level of trust. The more you can show your character outside of a classroom or office setting, the better.

**QUOTABLE:**

*"If people like you, they'll be your friend. If they trust you, they'll do business with you."*

—ZIG ZIGLAR

## GRADES

Want to know a crazy thing about networking? By networking well, you can get better grades in school. Yes, you can increase your GPA based on who you know and how you connect with them. Here's how:

- Do you spend time with students who succeed academically? Study with them or ask them to tutor you. Do you know upperclassmen who have taken your classes already? They may be able to provide hints about how the teacher grades or insights on the format of exams. If you need help, get it. Keep in mind that getting advice is quite different from getting answers. Student leaders do not cheat.

- Do you have good relationships with your teachers? Meet with teachers outside of class, participate, and show your interest in the subject. Being open with your teachers will only help you. Teachers often consider your effort and participation when grading. A good student/teacher relationship is also important when it comes to letters of recommendation down the road.

- Do you help others succeed? Return the favor and tutor your peers in your areas of strength. Going over the material with others will also help you to better understand the material yourself.

## ULTRA-INCLUSIVITY

Everyone around you has something to offer. Who you know and how you utilize your network may improve your life in ways you don't even foresee.[48] Great student leaders recognize this and place an emphasis on making a strong connection with everyone they meet.

Bill Clinton knew that a strong network would be essential when he ran for office. While he was a student at Georgetown, he wrote down

---

[48] When I was writing this, I couldn't help but think about the movie, Billy Madison. There is a scene in which Billy (Adam Sandler) calls the man he bullied in high school (Steve Buscemi) and apologizes. This phone call inadvertently saves Billy's life later in the movie – a funny example of the importance of relationships and networking.

the contact information of each person he met and followed up with those people to maintain positive relationships. Clinton valued the people around him, and he was rewarded later in life for his inclusive networking style by becoming the 42nd President of the United States.

Like Clinton, student leaders network with their classmates. They make good study buddies now and in the future they can help you professionally. Your peers will have jobs and can be a valuable resource to you down the road. Keep positive relationships so you don't walk into an interview and immediately get written off because your mortal enemy from high school works at the company and talks about you in a negative way. Make friends with people in your classes, especially in your major (college students). They will enter the workforce with you and could help you find the perfect job opportunity.

At the time of writing this, I spoke with Carter Cleaves – a high school Sophomore from Richland, Washington. He is an Eagle Scout and has already learned the importance of building a strong network and community. "A great leader is someone who is kind to everyone and never puts anyone out," he said. "Great leaders are inclusive and never leave anyone behind."

It is never too early to begin building your network. Whether your goal is to become an Eagle Scout or the President of the United States (or anything in between), every positive connection you create gets you one step closer.

Let's dig a little deeper on the specific networking items you'll need to master.

## UNDER-PROMISE, OVER-DELIVER

If you are consistently exceeding expectations, your network will notice. Think about my experience with Joe at AJ Bombers. All he promised initially was that I'd get one of their burgers. What I ended up getting was the opportunity of a lifetime to meet one of my favorite entrepreneurs at the time.

Exceeding expectations has everything to do with under-promising and over-delivering. Be confident enough to say "no" if expectations are too high – this way, you will never do the opposite: over-promise and under-deliver.

An example: you are involved in a sport and the coach asks if you can hold captain's practices twice a day, every day. You know it is not realistic to commit that much time, but could easily have one captain's practice every day. By being confident enough to tell the coach what you can realistically accomplish, you are tailoring expectations to better fit the reality of the situation. This way, if you *do* end up having captain's practices twice a day, you will have exceeded expectations and potentially impressed your coach.

### PRO TIP #6

Don't be like the person in Justin Timberlake's "Promises":
*"I know people make promises all the time / Then they turn right around and break them."*

Another example of this philosophy comes from the idea of the "crowded room". As a student, if you are organizing a meeting, you will most likely need to think about how many chairs you have available for the meeting. If you choose a large room to hold the meeting and have far more chairs than necessary, the room will feel empty. But if you choose a small room and some people have to stand through the meeting, the meeting will feel packed. It's all about establishing expectations. When people are asked later if a lot of people came to the meeting, it is better if they say, "Yeah, the room was packed," instead of, "Kind of, there were a lot of empty seats." These statements are strictly about perception. The packed room is far better because expectations were exceeded.

However, don't sell yourself short. Under-promising does not mean that you shouldn't push yourself. It simply means that you should be realistic about what you can deliver. You are capable of excellence and should hold yourself to high expectations.

## BECOME UNCOMFORTABLE

If you've watched the movie, "We Bought A Zoo," you may remember Benjamin Mee's[49] advice to his children:

> *You know, sometimes all you need is twenty seconds of insane courage. Just literally twenty seconds of just embarrassing bravery. And I promise you; something great will come of it.*

Reaching out to someone new is intimidating. Introducing yourself doesn't need to be fancy. A simple, "Hi, I'm Sarah" will do (unless your name is not Sarah; that would be pretty weird). The more you practice expanding your network, the better you will become at holding great initial conversations and cultivating your relationships.

## FOLLOW UP

Maintaining relationships takes effort. Send thank you notes all the time. There is never a bad time to write one (unless it is in reply to another thank you note – that may be a bit much). *Always* send thank you notes after interviews. Send them after helpful encounters with people in the community or if they've done something nice for you. These notes don't have to be long. An example of a thank you note is below:

"Dear (Blank),

*Thank you for writing me a letter of recommendation. I have really enjoyed having you as my literature and Shakespeare teacher this year and appreciate you taking the time to help in the application process for college. I also wanted to thank you for taking an interest in my college options and your helpful advice. I will let you know when I make my final decision.*

*Thanks again, and have a great winter break,*

*(Your name)*

---

[49] Played by Matt Damon, the greatest actor of this or any generation.

Even if the favor is small, a thank you card will always be appreciated. It can set the foundation for future relationships.

A quick note: in the example above, it is assumed that your teacher knows who you are. In other thank you notes, you may have to add a short reminder near the start by saying something like, "We met yesterday in your office and talked about the Green Bay Packers." It is important that this statement is brief but distinctive so they know exactly who you are; if it is too generic, they still may not remember you.

If you have never sent a thank you card for anything other than birthday presents, it is never too late to start. Go to the grocery store nearby and purchase a stack of them. Write one to someone who has done something for you in the past month, send it out, and see what comes of it. Sending a thank you note is a small gesture, but it can have a huge impact on what that person thinks of you.

> **QUOTABLE**
>
> *"The currency of real networking is not greed but generosity."*
>
> – KEITH FERRAZZI

## ARE YOU THAT GUY OR GIRL?

Some people network all wrong. I believe this is because they aren't working to *be* the right people – authentic, genuine, and real. When young people don't focus on filling their cup from the bottom, their default networking habits will not come across in the right ways. The items below are primary examples of networking faux pas that student leaders should avoid at all costs.

### The Wallflower

These are the people who never go out of their comfort zone at all. They tend to stick to corners of the room and avoid contact with people with whom they could be networking. Networking is not just for outgoing people. Everyone networks. Networking may not come as naturally to some, but it is achievable even if you're soft-spoken, shy, or uncomfortable.

### The "My Friends Are Cooler"

Everyone has friends. However, some people never leave their friend group to meet anyone new or different. This gives off the vibe that they are uninterested in connecting. Student leaders look for positive, diverse qualities in their networks, and the only way to achieve this is to expand your circle. When youth motivational speaker Houston Kraft was in high school, he created a kindness club. To be in the club you needed to try to do two things every day: 1. Meet someone new 2. Leave them better than you found them. Who have you met for the first time recently? Are they better because they met you?

### The Clinger

Everyone knows that person who is just "too much." These people tend to be overbearing and are not good networkers. Make strong connections, but also give space. Not everyone you meet needs to be a best friend.

### The Yes Man

Enthusiasm and involvement are great. But taking it too far and saying, "yes" to things you cannot commit to is horrible for networking. This goes back to the concept of under-promising and over-delivering. Only agree to what you can realistically accomplish.

### The Mooch

You know that friend that keeps asking you for money? The one that always wants a piece of your gum, but never gives you any in return? Moochers will take, take, take without providing any value in return. Networking is about *mutually* beneficial relationships. Make sure you aren't always the one asking for favors, referrals, and connections. Do your best to return favors, and be thankful when someone in your network helps you out.

The value of your network and how you utilize it can influence every aspect of your life. When you think about your goals, know that there will be 20 people between now and the time you achieve them that will help you out in big ways. *Nothing* of great value is accomplished alone. Take advantage of opportunities to network whenever you can.

As you continue reading, be sure to think about how each student leader characteristic also affects your relationship with your network. These lessons are not separate. We've discussed communicating well, building a personal brand, taking initiative, and managing projects effectively. Networking intertwines with each of these topics – your communication skills will help build your network; your personal brand will draw certain types of people to you; the actions you take to get out of your comfort zone will help your network thrive; projects become easier when the right group of people is working on them.

As we continue, don't forget to take aspects of all of these chapters and mold them into a leadership style that works for you.

I'd like to end this chapter with a few x's and o's of *how* to put your networking knowledge to work.

## FIRST IMPRESSIONS. LASTING IMPRESSIONS.

*While a book should not be judged by its cover, few people will pick it up if it is not inviting.*

—Unknown

Imagine you get a donut from the bakery and after your first bite you absolutely hate it. It tastes like a mix between carrots, broccoli, and gasoline. It is the worst donut you've ever had. Do you think you'd take a second bite of the donut? My guess is no, but hey, maybe you like torturing yourself.

Just like a donut, others' first encounter with you should be positive and leave them wanting more.

Some donuts taste so good it is impossible to put them down.

Have you ever been around someone you just can't get enough of? I'm certain this person made a positive impression the very first time you met each other.[50]

As the saying goes, you never get a second chance to make a good first impression. The initial view an individual has of you can help or hurt you whether you are interviewing for a job, at a networking event, or even making a new friend. Your appearance and mannerisms are important. Student leaders are aware of the message they are sending at first glance.

You've already learned that interviewers make a decision on whether they will hire someone within seven seconds of meeting them. If you don't make a good first impression, you don't get the job – plain and simple.

Outside of interviews, if you would like to get more people to your sporting event, raise more money for a school trip, or introduce yourself to that special someone[51], you'll want to master the art of the first impression. Not everyone will take the time to get to know you. Ohio State University assistant professor Robert Lount claims, "First impressions matter when you want to build a lasting trust. If you get off on the wrong foot, the relationship may never be completely right again."

So how do you make a great first impression?

## INTERPERSONAL SKILLS

Within the chapter on communication, I set the stage for communication to be viewed as a whole. However, there are very specific nonverbals that you'll need to master when meeting someone for the first time.

---

[50] And if not, I'm sure they had a steep uphill climb after your first meeting to win you over.

[51] Bae (or your potential next significant other) wants you to make a good first impression.

According to an article in Business Insider, "During face to face meetings, 93% of people's judgments of others are based on non-verbal input." Below are the big ones to keep in mind.

### Smile

Before you even say hello to someone, make yourself approachable. A smile can make the people around you feel comfortable. People will be more eager to meet you if you appear friendly and confident. Part of this is your posture and body language as well – stand up straight, look people in the eye, and relax. Even if you don't feel confident, stand like it – and more often than not, you'll have people fooled. A smile can show people you're worth connecting with and is a refreshing break from negativity.

**PRO TIP #7**

Fake it (to become it). Olympic long-jumper Jackie Joyner-Kersee maintains that smiling before a race will alleviate stress and make you a better competitor. Acting confident, even if you're not, can alleviate stress and make you more approachable.

### Eye Contact

Eye contact is an indicator of confidence. A lack of eye contact can indicate shyness or disinterest to the person you're talking to. If you're nervous, try actively thinking about the eye color of the individual you're speaking with. On the flip side, staring at the person is interpreted as aggressive and creepy. Relax, focus on what the person is saying, and the eye contact should come naturally.

### Handshake

When meeting someone for the first time, stand and extend your right hand. Make eye contact and offer a greeting during the handshake, including the other person's name and a pleasantry: "I'm glad to meet you, Mrs. Anderson." A good handshake is firm, but not bone-crushing; a limp and flimsy handshake gives the impression of weakness. It should last about three seconds, and is usually "pumped" twice from the elbow. Practice this with friends, professors, or your current employer to get honest feedback.

You should also be aware of the moisture on your hands before you shake. No one wants to get slimed by sweaty hands. To make sure your handshake isn't a wet one, use hand sanitizer: the alcohol in it has a natural drying effect on your hands. If you have no hand sanitizer, don't fret – you can always subtly brush your hand off on your pants as you walk.

### Posture

Sitting or standing up straight projects strength and confidence. Slouching in your chair makes you seem lazy, uninterested and even arrogant. On the other hand, leaning too far forward comes across as aggressive. Keep your shoulders back, chest out, and sit near the end of your chair. The same goes for standing— keep your knees straight (but don't faint!) and relax your hands to your sides.

**PRO TIP #8**

*Do a power pose before attempting something nerve-wracking. Put your arms up in the air like you just won a race, or do the "muscle-man" pose. Hold the pose for a little. You can trick your body into performing better and being more confident. (You may want to do this in private, depending on your level of confidence.)*

### Follow-up Questions

Going up to someone, particularly an authority figure, for the first time can be intimidating, but being prepared with a smile, introduction, and follow-up questions can prevent the conversation from lulling. A simple, "How did you get into that field?" or "What is the best part about what you do?" goes a long way. Have a few in your back pocket to avoid awkward silences.

First impressions stick. Studies show that every time you see another person, you remember the snap judgment you made upon the first meeting— at least until you start building a relationship with that person. In most cases, you won't get the opportunity to do so if you do not have a positive initial interaction.

Recognize the importance of a great first impression. Put time and energy into polishing your initial encounters with others because they make a big difference. Will you look confident or insecure? Friendly or antisocial? By preparing well, showing confidence through good eye contact, smiling, and giving a winning handshake, you will set yourself apart right from the start. Don't ruin your chances of making a great connection in the first few seconds. Be that delicious glazed donut that makes it impossible for someone to forget you.[52]

> **QUOTABLE**
>
> *"Being able to have a conversation with anyone, even someone you just met is an underrated skill; it makes everyone feel more confident and comfortable."*
>
> — ALYSSA COMINS
> FORMER WI DECA STATE OFFICER

As a student leader, always remember your network will affect your life in ways currently unknown to you.

The strength of your network can assist in your career, grades, and general well-being (why would you not want to grow it?). We'll talk later about maintaining these relationships, but following the tips outlined in this chapter will put you well on your way to *thinking* like a leader and then naturally, as your thoughts turn to actions, *becoming* one.

---

[52] PS – I never thought I'd be telling people to "Be a Donut," but in this scenario it just kind of worked.

## CHAPTER 5 ACTION PACKED DISCUSSION QUESTIONS

1. *How can you expand your network?*

2. *What are three ways you can strengthen the connections you already have?*

3. *List three people you could network with in school or in the community.*

4. *How do people perceive you upon meeting you?*

5. *How can you polish your personal brand to improve your first impression?*

Chapter 6 Preface
# NO HICE LA TAREA

I will never forget the day in high school that I knowingly didn't complete a Spanish assignment. I was a very conscientious student in high school, and on that day, I could feel the disappointment of my teacher as she collected papers and I had nothing to turn in.

But there was a reason I didn't do it, and I've thought about this from time-to-time as a metaphor for a lot of other occasions in my life.

There were only a few days left in the semester, and I walked into the classroom with a smile on my face.

Prior to this day, I had always completed my assignments, not just in Spanish, but in every class I'd ever taken. I'm not saying I was a perfect student, but I was usually pretty on top of things. This day, I knew about the assignment, I weighed my options, and I flat-out made the decision not to do it.

I remember looking at my Spanish teacher as she collected the work, "I didn't do it."

She looked at me, eyebrows furrowed, "Que?"

I didn't know a lot of Spanish, but I knew enough to tell her I didn't do the homework. "No hice la tarea."

My Spanish name in high school was Bonafacio.[53] She gave me a disappointed look and said, "Bonafacio? Por que no?"

I just shrugged and said, "I didn't have time."

She got very upset with me and told me that I needed to take this more seriously and finish my assignments or my grade would suffer.

I nodded and told her that I understood.

Could I have finished the assignment? Definitely. Why did I choose not to finish it?

I had two tests the same day in classes where my overall grade was either going to get higher or lower based on how I did on the tests.

I also had an away basketball game the night before which limited my time even further.

Being so close to the end of the semester, I knew that the one Spanish assignment I missed was going to have no overall effect on my final grade.

So I organized my priorities, and my Spanish assignment just didn't make the cut.

I looked at the time I had and chose to place an emphasis on the things that mattered most.

Sure, I could have stayed up until 3 AM and finished the Spanish assignment, but again, I knew that sleeping well the night before a test was an important piece of good test preparation.

The one thing I would have done differently is better explain the situation to my Spanish teacher. She had every right to be upset with me; she thought I was blowing off her class! She also showed an interest in helping me keep my grades up which teachers ought

---

[53] I have no idea why. Don't ask.

to do. She had no idea that I had thought a lot about it and made the decision carefully (because, let's be honest, most students who don't turn in assignments aren't missing them because they have their priorities straight).

I believe old people will try to tell young people at every turn what their priorities *should* be. But some of the best young leaders I've ever met *know* their priorities, and have moved their lives in incredible directions because they stay true to their priorities at all costs.

As a student, you will need to make decisions every day on how you spend your time. You will need to take a hard look at what is important and what is not, and you will need to go all in on some things and choose to let go of others.

Listo?[54]

This chapter will teach you the ins-and-outs of time management. I'll talk about:

- Understanding time
- Establishing priorities
- Jumping in, avoiding distractions, and taking brain breaks
- Organization and flexibility

---

[54] This means "Ready?" in Spanish.

Chapter 6

# TIME MANAGEMENT

*"The time will pass anyway; we might just as well put that passing time to the best possible use."*

– Earl Nightingale[55]

Ever feel like there aren't enough hours in the day? You definitely wouldn't be the only one. It seems to me that the human race in general has a love-hate relationship with time. Most of us think we never have enough of it while we spend most of our moments awake actively wasting it.

This book is about leadership – and more specifically, about how the way we *think* about anything can drastically influence what we *do*.

Leading others to accomplish meaningful goals takes a lot of energy in the area of effectively managing time. Students who prioritize and remove distractions can complete tasks far more successfully. Just as I pointed out in the introduction way back at the start of this book – this

---

[55] An author and motivational speaker, known as "The Dean of Professional Development."

is not exactly rocket science. It should be pretty obvious that young people who aren't as *distracted* will become more *focused*, and through a higher level of *focus*, can accomplish more.

Achieving this natural advantage has everything to do with how we *think* about our *time*.

Before we dive into strategies that will help us manage our time effectively, we need to make sure we're fully understanding time – what it is and why it is so valuable. Then we can look at ways in which we can maximize the time we have.

I want to be as clear and simple as possible. You have the capacity to do anything you want with your time, and your choices will define you.

Do you remember this image from earlier in the book?[56]

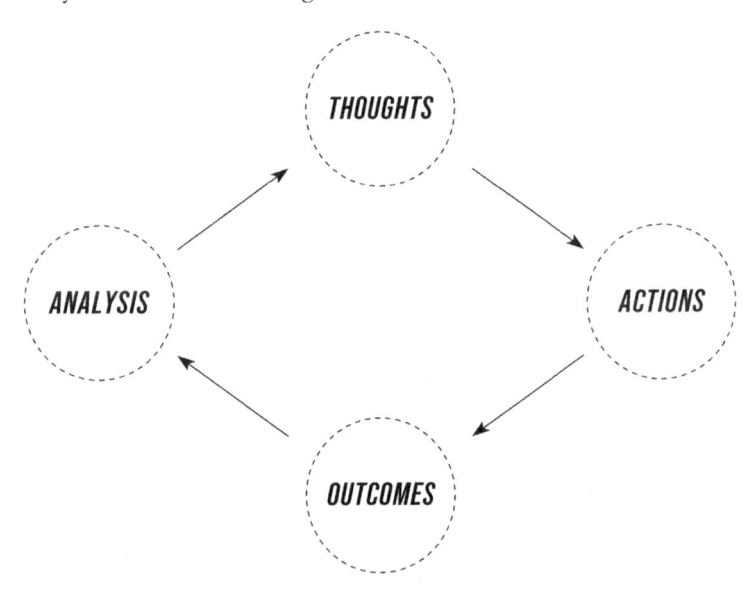

```
         THOUGHTS
        ↗         ↘
  ANALYSIS         ACTIONS
        ↖         ↙
         OUTCOMES
```

Unfortunately, in the real world, our thoughts can have a tendency to push us in the wrong direction – hence the need for this book. For a lot of young people, the framework above can turn into something like this:

---

[56] If not, that's okay. It's literally right here.

## Diagram

**THOUGHTS**
- "I SHOULD NEVER TRY AT ANYTHING"
- "I CAN'T DO ANYTHING RIGHT"
- "I'M NOT GOOD ENOUGH"
- OVERTHINKING
- UNHELPFUL QUESTIONING

**DISTRACTIONS / ACTIONS**
- SELF DOUBT
- ANXIETY
- FEAR
- DESPAIR
- SECOND-GUESSING
- "I CAN'T DO IT."
- HIDING WHO I REALLY AM
- UNHEALTHY DECISIONS
- NOT DOING SOMETHING I KNOW I SHOULD
- HOLDING MYSELF BACK
- TRYING TO BE "COOL"

**OUTCOMES**
- GOT IN TROUBLE
- PRETENDED I DIDN'T CARE
- REGRET
- DIDN'T ACT LIKE MYSELF

**ANALYSIS**
- "NOTHING EVER GOES MY WAY"
- DIDN'T GET WHAT I WANTED

---

Do you see how distractions and negative emotions can hijack our lives?

The "analysis" portion of the negative example above will simply create worse thoughts, worse actions, and worse outcomes. The choices we make from the inside out have the ability to spiral throughout our lives.

Our consistent thoughts begin to define us over time.

Why do we allow ourselves to get so distracted and pulled away from the person we truly want to become?

Think of some of the examples young people do every day:

- » Work on the computer with a phone face up in front of them
- » Keep twenty tabs open at once on an internet browser
- » Switch between writing that paper last-minute and checking social media
- » Check a phone anytime an emotion pops up

What we are doing is undercutting the value of our time. The amount of time we spend in positive thought will have lasting effects on our lives. The same can be said about our time in negative thought. Distracted thought is similar to negative thought in that we are not intentionally working to think and be a leader.

I believe most of us aren't fully aware of the value of our time. In this chapter, we're going to dive into what time truly is and how we can make the most of it to become the best version of ourselves.

## UNDERSTANDING TIME

An article from Entrepreneur Magazine suggests that there are two types of time: clock time and real time, and that you can't manage your time until you understand the difference between the two.

***Clock time*** never changes.

It constantly moves at the same pace, and you cannot control it. No matter what you are doing, there are 60 seconds in a minute, 60 minutes in an hour, 24 hours in a day, and so on. When you turn 25, that will be your age in "clock time."

***Real time*** is what you actually live in.

Time speeds up or slows down depending on the activity you are engaged in. The classes you take are always the same length in clock time, but somehow, they seem much longer in the days right before summer break. You sleep (hopefully) around seven hours each night – but it feels like no time at all compared to the seven hours you spend at school.

It is absolutely imperative for young people to operate in real time.

When we grow old and look back on our lives, we will not remember a minute-by-minute play-by-play of everything that happened – our brains literally can't recall everything in clock time. We will remember moments. Some moments will have been ten seconds and felt like 10 hours, and some will have been days and only felt like minutes. To be clear, these moments had more to do with how we *thought* and *felt* about what was happening than the time passing on a clock.

This is why it is so important to manage how we *think* about time.

We *should* feel grateful for the time we have.

We *should* allow moments to excite us and energize us.

We *should* learn that living in the present (without distraction) will maximize our real time experience.

We *should* be working to maximize moments that bring us joy or lead us to high levels of long-term satisfaction.

We *should* think about time as something we *get to experience*, not simply in the ticks of a hand on a clock.

Unfortunately, quite often we do the exact opposite.

We take the most time to do the homework we hate.

We make moments of discomfort feel longer by checking our phones, watches, or clocks and counting the minutes.

We ask questions like *are we there yet* and *how much longer is this going to take* instead of recognizing just how special our time in the present moment is.[57]

For some odd reason, it seems like we are actually *trying* to maximize the most *undesirable* moments in our day.

We need a major shift in how we think about our time.

The next time you have to do a homework assignment you're not passionate about – just sit down and get it done. Remove all distractions and do it, because what you're really doing by completing it quickly and without complaint is minimizing the *real time* effect this assignment has on your day.

---

[57] I am often times guilty of this too. It is so incredibly difficult to stay present in the moment and know that clock time doesn't have to define my experiences.

Spoiler alert – you don't make your life any better by taking longer to complain about a task than the time it would have actually taken you to complete it.

There are specific things you can do to maximize your *real time* experience. We're going to get into them now, but before we do, take a moment to commit to living in the present and *feeling moments* as opposed to simply looking at a clock for your updates on time.

Here's how to make the most out of real time:

## ESTABLISH PRIORITIES

This directly relates to my experience in Spanish class. Students are making internal decisions about priorities every day. Watch Netflix or write my paper? Stay up late or get a good night's sleep? Study for the exam ahead of time or cram the night before (or day of)? The answers to these questions play a huge role in separating students from student leaders.

There are four categories that a task or project can fall into according to its urgency and importance (as you can see on the following chart). Students often confuse the urgent for the important, but student leaders understand how to separate the two and manage them well. As the academic, extracurricular, and personal tasks pile up, try to organize your tasks and address them in order, from Quadrant I on down.

**Urgent** tasks need to be accomplished soon. They are at the top of to-do lists because there is an impending deadline. What I've found while researching for this book is that most high school students' idea of "urgent," is actually not urgent at all. Think hard about this category before you throw *responding to an e-mail* into the *Urgent* category.

**Important** tasks are ones that will have the greatest impact on you. They make the largest difference in the big picture of what you're trying to accomplish.

Can you think of examples in your own life for each quadrant?

The following is a framework for managing priorities effectively.

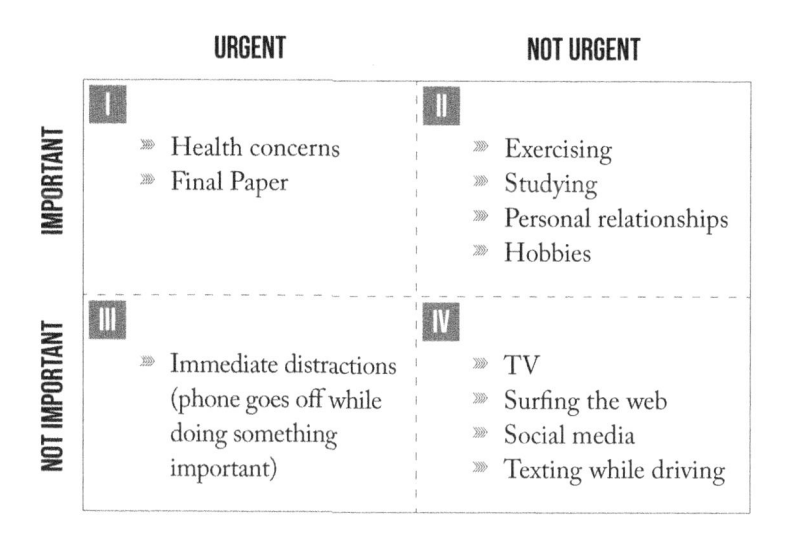

|  | **URGENT** | **NOT URGENT** |
|---|---|---|
| **IMPORTANT** | **I**<br>» Health concerns<br>» Final Paper | **II**<br>» Exercising<br>» Studying<br>» Personal relationships<br>» Hobbies |
| **NOT IMPORTANT** | **III**<br>» Immediate distractions (phone goes off while doing something important) | **IV**<br>» TV<br>» Surfing the web<br>» Social media<br>» Texting while driving |

*Quadrant I:* Urgent and Important tasks should be addressed first. These are both pressing *and* have a significant impact on your life and goals. You can often eliminate things from ever falling into this category by working ahead.

*Quadrant II:* Tasks that are Important but Not Urgent exist here. Try to spend most of your time in this quadrant, as it contributes most to your well-being and overall success. If you spend your time studying throughout the semester, it will prevent you from studying all night for your final exam the day before you have to take it. Too often, the pressure of deadlines pushes us out of this quadrant and into Quadrant I.

QUOTABLE:

*"The essence of self-discipline is to do the important thing rather than the urgent thing."*

—BARRY WERNER

*Quadrant III:* Urgent but Not Important tasks take up much of our time as well. These are called distractions. This quadrant often feels like Quadrant I because of the pressure of deadlines. Spending too much time in this quadrant causes you to feel as though you work and work but get nothing done at the end of the day.

*Quadrant IV:* Finally, there are tasks that are neither Urgent nor Important. We do not need to cut Quadrant IV activities out of our lives completely, but we should ideally be spending no more than 5%-

10% of our time in this quadrant. (To put things in perspective: one hour is 4% of your 24-hour day.) At least during the week, try to spend as little time here as possible. Work to spend a good percentage of your time in Quadrant II.

## DEVELOP A PLAN

Have you ever seen *The Amazing Race*? The teams that get moving without making a plan are typically not the winners. Instead, they have to backtrack and waste time.

You must have a plan of action before jumping thoughtlessly into an endeavor. Establishing a plan consists of setting goals (see the chapter on Project Management), working with others, and setting personal checkpoints to keep yourself on task.

## JUMP IN

> *"Take time to deliberate; but when the time for action arrives, stop thinking and go in."*
>
> —Napoleon Bonaparte

Once a plan has been established, don't waste time getting started.

Starting is the hardest part. Procrastination should be arrested for killing productivity. Nothing good comes from delaying work you will have to do anyway. This simply extends the *real time* feeling of the work itself. Develop a plan and jump in. Letting procrastination become a habit will cause you a lot of stress. You'll also have much less time for your important, Quadrant II activities.

## AVOID DISTRACTIONS

While distractions may be inevitable at times, look to minimize them as best you can. When researching something online, it's easy to open a new tab and get lost in Facebook or Twitter. Push yourself to stay focused. It's easy to check your phone every time you get a notification. Recognize the value in leaving it unopened until you are on a planned break.

A lot of students claim that constantly checking their phone and listening to music while working is just multitasking: "I'm a good multitasker, so I can do x, y, and z *while* I write my paper!"

### PRO TIP #9

With cell phones – which also serve as social media outlets – it's out of sight, out of mind. Do not keep your phone face-up next to you as you study. Keep it in a pocket of your backpack, or leave it across the room so that it takes more effort for you to check it. Allow yourself to get up to check it only once an hour, or after every chapter of reading or section of homework.

The truth is: no one multitasks well.

In a study done by Fast Company, adults working in professional offices were studied to see how often they were interrupted, and what the consequences of these breaks in their work were. Every three minutes, on average, the workers took brief breaks to do something unrelated: check their e-mail, go on eBay, or make a phone call.

So, what's the big deal?

All of these mini-breaks (also known as multitasking) decreased the overall productivity of the workers. When they shifted from activity to activity, their whole line of thinking also shifted. Their ability to think abstractly and be productive also became extremely limited. The study showed it took their minds an average of *twenty-three* minutes to get back on task.

Multitasking causes us to work faster to compensate for all the in-between time-wasters. Trying to work at a faster pace compromises the quality of our work and makes us more stressed. Although taking breaks may seem like a short amount of time in our day, they have *real consequences* in how efficiently we get stuff done.

## WORK IN BLOCKS

Focus is a skill that can be developed over time. Have you ever fallen asleep while reading? (I know I have.) The more you read, the more your mind is conditioned to do it for long periods of time. This is why some people can read for hours while others fall asleep after ten minutes. It has nothing to do with skill, but with practice. The same is true for studying, working, or concentrating on any one task. With a little time and effort, you can condition your mind to focus when you need it to.

A great way to extend your focus is to work in blocks. If your mind wanders after reading for ten minutes, set a timer for ten minutes and read without interruption until the timer goes off. Then, take a quick break (more on this in a moment) before setting your timer again. Push yourself for twelve minutes this time. Continue to push yourself to work for longer periods of time by establishing uninterrupted blocks – you'll be surprised how much you can accomplish.

## TAKE BRAIN BREAKS

Like a muscle, your brain needs a break now and again. Reward yourself with a "brain break" after working for a certain amount of time or after completing an assignment.

University of Illinois professor, Alejandro Lleras, says "constant stimulation is registered by our brains as unimportant, to the point that the brain erases it from our awareness."

By continuing to do a task for an extended period of time, your brain will essentially stop processing information as a new stimulus. Take a break every once and awhile (without procrastinating) to rejuvenate your brain and make yourself more productive.

Approach these breaks with purpose. Brain breaks are planned, distractions are not. Below are some short breaks you can take to rejuvenate your mind.

- Take a walk. Even if it is around the library, the movement will get your blood flowing and reenergize you for another block of time.
- Get a snack. It's less about the eating and more about the break. You don't have to be very hungry to eat an apple. It's best to only eat while you're on a planned break – continuously snacking as you work serves more as a distraction than a snack. Try to stick to healthy foods in order to feel sharp.

> **PRO TIP #10**
>
> Don't study in the same place you relax. Your bedroom is likely full of distractions. And unless you're just reading, don't study in your bed. Find a clean space where you can sit up, spread out, and be diligent.

- Check your phone. Respond to those texts that you've waited until your break to check. Make a call. Send a selfie or two. This is the time to do it.
- Change your scenery. During a break, sometimes finding a different place can help you concentrate. Staying in the same place long enough might lull you into being unproductive.

## STAY ORGANIZED

In video games, this would be just like saving your game. If you always had to start from the beginning, you would never get very far. Be sure you are always organized enough to build off the progress you've made.

One way to do this is to keep a planner. Whether it's electronic or physical, a planner will help you remember deadlines and stay current with to-do lists. At the beginning of the week, plan out everything you need to get done. Prioritize (according to the tasks' urgency and importance), and plan out a schedule for completing each task.

Another way to stay organized is by keeping a binder or folder for each of your classes.[58] This way, less time is spent looking for assignments or

---

[58] You can also keep digital folders to stay organized online.

work, and more time is spent completing the work. It will also reduce stress and the frantic where-is-my-homework freak-out.

---

*Remember when your teacher handed you those planners at the beginning of the school year and preached you needed to utilize this organizational tool in order to be successful? Well, we all know half of us throw those away or lose them about halfway through the year, and the other half of us probably forget about even writing anything down in those useless journals that add more weight in our backpack as we walk to our classes. But then there is the day we forget when a big project is due, or the date of an important meeting. It's an embarrassing and disappointing moment when we realize we've forgotten it. By working smarter and taking advantage of organizational tools, we can become the stronger and more efficient leader.*

*I'm the type of person who believes my memory works like a computer, where I can just press "control h" and have a history of all the dates and assignments I have to do, but in reality, I don't, and I forget a lot more than I actually admit. As an incoming high school senior, my whole high school and middle school career has been a battle of managing dance rehearsals, sports, meetings for multiple school clubs, and still finding time to fit in homework, spending time with family and friends, and of course, the essentials: eating and sleeping.*

*By adding an agenda to my daily life, I have a constant reminder of what I have to do for that day and what I have planned for the next day, week, or month in advance. I also hang a large calendar on my wall, which again, gives me the constant reminder of my schedule, but if I have something really important I need to remember, I stick a bright, colorful sticky note onto my calendar so I know I won't forget to look at it. With a little bit of organization, my life has changed from mess to success.*

*Even though we see ourselves as independent individuals, sometimes a small dependence on a simple organization tool, like an agenda, can lift a burden off our shoulders and make a huge difference. Working smarter can turn your career, if not your life, around.*

—Becky Carlson
Former Michigan FCCLA State Officer

## BE FLEXIBLE

Even though your goal should be to stick to the schedule, sometimes the unexpected happens. You may find yourself spending a little more time on a task than you expected. Accept the fact that you cannot always make a flawless plan. Be able to alter your schedule accordingly when a situation calls for it.

・・・

Whether it be studying for tests and completing your homework or doing well at your future job, knowing how to effectively use your time is vital.

You will face deadlines, probably more than one at a time, and your work will pile up. Don't get frazzled; take a step back and attack it.

Think about time management from a student leader perspective, and work on maximizing your *real time* experience every day by living in the present and being grateful for the time you get.

Use the tips in this chapter to help you manage your time effectively.

## CHAPTER 7 ACTION PACKED DISCUSSION QUESTIONS

*1. What are a few examples of your Quadrant I, II, III, and IV activities?*

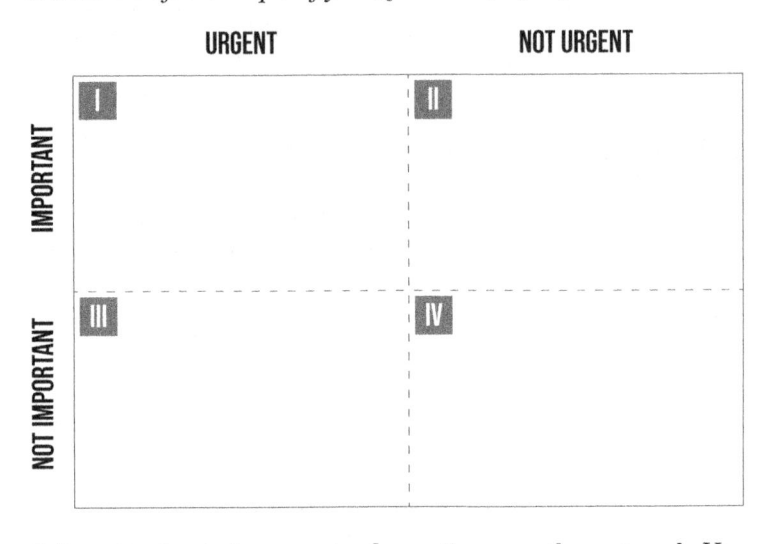

|  | **URGENT** | **NOT URGENT** |
|---|---|---|
| **IMPORTANT** | I | II |
| **NOT IMPORTANT** | III | IV |

*2. Pay attention to how you spend your time over the next week. How much time do you spend in each quadrant?*

_____

_____

*3. How can you regulate the time spent in Quadrant IV (not urgent and not important)?*

_____

_____

*4. Where can you study to avoid distractions?*

_____

Chapter 7 Preface
# THERE'S GOT TO BE A BETTER WAY

When I was a freshman in college, I had a professor who made my life very difficult.

The man must have been around 80 years old, and I'm convinced he believed he needed to cover everything in the entire textbook every class period. His pace was blisteringly fast and none of it seemed to be organized into any particular order. There just seemed to be lots of words chosen randomly to form sentences that didn't make much sense.

If his way of presenting information wasn't bad enough, he would accompany his lectures with PowerPoints – every PowerPoint he'd present had about 300 slides and each slide had several paragraphs of about 300 words in 8-point font.

Looking through his PowerPoints was like looking through the Terms and Conditions when signing up for Spotify - you won't understand most of it, and it would take most of your life to read it all.

As the day of our first exam approached, I was freaking out.

I asked several of my friends what they were studying and they were just as clueless. Actually, many of them were much more clueless because they had stopped attending the class altogether because our professor didn't take attendance.

I started looking through the PowerPoints and going through the textbook. There was way too much information. After hours of forcing my eyes to glaze over in his PowerPoints, it became very clear to me that I had no chance of doing well on this test.

Then a lightbulb went on. I thought, *there's got to be a better way*.

I decided I needed to try something different. Honestly, anything would have probably been better than continuing to fall asleep on printouts of his PowerPoints.[59]

After thinking about my options, I decided (in spite of my feelings towards this boring old man) to send him an e-mail explaining that I could use some assistance studying for the exam.

He e-mailed me back almost immediately and asked me to stop by his office later that day; now I really freaked out. I'd love to tell you that I'm just such a personable individual that I can get along with anyone and not be nervous, but the thought of sitting one-on-one with this professor who seemed to be torturing me with every lecture scared me to death.

My options were either to come up with an excuse to not sit down with him, or face my fear and join him.

After some internal debate, I decided my grade on the exam was too important to not try everything and found myself walking into his office later that day.

I was ready to tell him how unprepared I felt and how stressful it was to be studying for an impossible exam, but to my surprise, he started the conversation and everything changed.

---

[59] Plus, my drool started to smear the ink on the PowerPoint pages.

"Hi Kyle, I'm glad you came in. Please, have a seat. You know, I'm surprised more people don't come in for my office hours. We cover a lot of information in class, and I'm sure studying for the exam is difficult. How can I help you do well on this?"

Whoa.

Not what I was expecting.

We spent the next hour going through important pieces of information from his lessons. He didn't give me answers, but he gave me direction which was more than enough. I left his office feeling relaxed and comfortable.

Later that evening, I got out the PowerPoints and the textbook, studied for an hour and felt ready to hit a home run.

I'd be lying if I told you I could remember exactly what I got on the exam, but I do remember I wasn't disappointed. The information coming from my professor's office hours helped me a great deal, and I went to see him before every future exam that semester.

This was just one example of working smarter.

As my classmates were making guesses about what to study, I went straight to the source.

There have been plenty of moments in my life in which I look back and think, "I could have done that better." I'm continuously learning that there is always a "better way."

In this chapter, I'll provide the high-level ways to *think* about *working smarter*, but it's up to you to find ways to *do it* every day.

You certainly have the opportunity every day to find ways to *work smarter*.

In this scenario, I could have spent a lot more time doing unproductive studying when one hour with my professor made all the difference.

This chapter is the closest thing to a *short cut* we can find in building lives we can be proud of – it is about finding ways to do things in one hour that may take others ten hours. It is about being both *efficient* and *effective*.

In this chapter I'll talk about:

- The art of delegation
- Monitoring your kryptonite
- Continuous improvement
- Synergy

Chapter 7

# WORKING SMARTER

*"A smart man makes a mistake, learns from it, and never makes that mistake again. But a wise man finds a smart man and learns from him how to avoid the mistake altogether."*

—Roy H. Williams

As a student leader, you'll probably have more responsibilities than the average student. It's part of the gig. And responsibilities are a great thing – it's how we learn, grow, get involved, meet people, and accomplish things. It's certainly better to be busy than bored. But there's no reason to do more work than needed. By working smarter, you can reserve more time for friends, hobbies, fun, or even achieving more than you initially expected.

## EMPOWERING OTHERS THROUGH DELEGATION

Delegation is a difficult art to master, and one that is vital to your success as a student leader. I touched on this topic briefly in the Project Management chapter, but I wanted to make sure you know exactly what this is and how you can use it as a student leader.

Put simply, *delegation* is when a leader assigns tasks to followers, with the end goal of the team in mind. It does not involve asking others to take on tasks that you don't feel like doing yourself or being demanding. It does involve trusting members of your team with important tasks and *empowering* them to accomplish these tasks for the good of the team. Nothing worth accomplishing can be done alone. Delegating tasks makes a group more efficient, fosters teamwork, and reduces stress.

> **QUOTABLE**
>
> *"Nothing worth accomplishing can be done alone."*

It takes the *right* type of leadership to *delegate* well. Think back to our soccer goalie, Ben. He was constantly thinking about the good of the team – *what will it take for our team to be successful?* We all saw this on a consistent basis so when Ben would delegate work to us or tell us we needed to work harder we knew it wasn't from a selfish perspective; it was because he cared about all of our overall success.

Here are a few tips to help you *become* the type of leader who *delegates* effectively:

### Buy In

Followers will only complete tasks if they have bought in to the larger goal. If you are trying to raise money for a cause, you must first get your followers to buy into the idea that the cause is a worthy one. The more people care, the more they will be willing to help out when asked.

### Start Early

Getting people involved early will make them feel more invested in the project as time goes on. People support what they help to create.

### Provide Detail

Delegation does not work if you have not provided enough direction. Similar to setting SMART goals, you will need to establish specific expectations and deadlines with those you are working with. If a task has been delegated to you, ask your leader for the specifics. Clarity will make a huge difference as the outcomes typically mirror the expectations. There's a well-known saying: "The devil is in the details." Anything worth doing must be done thoroughly.

### Check In

Nothing is worse than reaching a deadline only to hear a team member say, "Oh, I never did that." Checking in from time to time will remove the risk of this happening. Think of yourself as a GPS system. Someone else is still driving the car; you are just making sure they stay on course until they reach the desired destination.[60]

### Give Praise

Make sure others are recognized for the hard work they have put in; this is a good idea even if you're not the leader. If they do all the work and you get all the praise, people won't be invested – and why would they be? But if you make it about them, their contributions, and what the team is accomplishing others will be more interested and involved. Be sure to give credit to those who have put effort in. A little praise goes a long way.

QUOTABLE:

*"It is amazing what can be accomplished when no one cares who gets the credit."*

—HARRY TRUMAN

## MONITOR YOUR KRYPTONITE

What are some low priority items that suck up your time and energy? The tasks or activities that are easy for you to spend hours doing but don't increase your overall productivity or happiness. Netflix? Gaming? Your cell phone?

---

[60] And every now and then you may need to recognize they are off track and provide them with a "rerouting" notification.

For me, I can hit the snooze button about 15 times before actually getting out of bed in the morning. Most of the time this just makes me feel groggier and doesn't increase my productivity or happiness at all.

I consider these things *kryptonite*.

In the literal sense *kryptonite* is the one material that can defeat Superman. For the purposes of this book *kryptonite* is the one thing that can defeat student leaders.

As "put-together" as young people try to be, they still have shortcomings and areas that need improvement.[61]

Some questions to ask yourself to define your *kryptonite*:

- Do you spend too much time on your phone?
- Could time spent playing video games be used more productively?
- Do certain friends consistently distract you from getting work done?
- Does unhealthy snacking while studying have a negative impact on your life?

Sometimes our *kryptonite* can be small, as in, "I just watched the whole first season of The Office because I was bored."

Sometimes our *kryptonite* can be big, as in, "I seek out alcohol when I am feeling stressed."

Either way, learning to manage your *kryptonite* while you're young can potentially save you from years and years of lost productivity or happiness.

I'm not implying by any stretch of the imagination that managing *kryptonite* is easy – that's why I call it *kryptonite* in the first place. Everyone in the world has destructive forces working to pull them away from the direction of greatest happiness. It is important you know you are not alone in your battle against your *kryptonite*, whatever it may be.

---

[61] Don't we all?

A few suggestions that may help you manage your *kryptonite*:

- Find a trustworthy accountability partner who will be honest with you and keep you on the right path.
- Talk with a trusted adult about your *kryptonite*. This can be scary, but sharing your truth is so important in managing unproductive actions.
- Become self-aware; ask yourself questions about what triggers your *kryptonite* behaviors. Practice breathing, being silent for a moment, or meditating to calm yourself when you feel pulled to engage in your *kryptonite* actions.

It would be unrealistic to simply tell you, "You know that thing that is hard for you to overcome? That thing that takes away from your overall happiness or productivity? Just stop doing that."

Instead, try to become fully aware of your *kryptonite*. Self-awareness must come before progress. My hope at the end of the day is that you get to the point in which your current *kryptonite* becomes a small memory of a distraction you overcame.

## GET BETTER

***The best way to work smarter is to get smarter.*** By continuing to learn and improve, student leaders are consistently looking to get better at whatever it is they are working on.

Think about driving somewhere for the first time. You may go the route you think will be fastest, and get there just fine. Imagine that you have to drive to this same place every day for the next two weeks. You may test out different routes, and by the end of the two weeks, you have found the quickest route possible.

It is the same in student leadership.

Seeking the best way to complete tasks, delegate, or manage time takes practice and patience. Student leaders know where they are now is not where they should be one, five, or ten years from now.

The only way to get where you want to be is by getting better every day. By learning, growing, and constantly pursuing improvement, student leaders always work to find the best route to their desired destination.

## SHARPEN THE AXE

Similar to what you read in the chapter on Time Management, taking breaks can help you *work smarter*.

In his book, *The 7 Habits of Highly Effective People*, Steven Covey tells the story of a woodcutter whose axe gets duller as time passes, but he continues cutting down trees. If the woodcutter were to stop sawing, sharpen his saw, and go back to cutting the tree with a fresh blade, he would actually save time and effort in the long run. Your brain is the axe in this example. If you've been focused too hard for too long, you may need to take a break to figuratively *sharpen your axe*.

Be careful not to confuse a productive, planned break with distractions and multitasking. The axe doesn't get any sharper if the break is simply a distraction.

## SYNERGY

I tend to talk about *synergy* as being when the *sum is greater than the individual parts*.

The idea of synergy is this: more can be accomplished when teams work well together than if each member of the team worked alone.

An example of synergy might be Henry Ford inventing the assembly line to be more efficient or the idea in sports that even the best player can't beat the best team. Student leaders not only promote synergy, but work hard to practice it in all group settings.

Below is an example. Don't worry; it's really not about the math.

This is what we'd expect:

2+2+2+2+2=10

But with synergy, this is what could happen:

2+2+2+2+2=1,000

In math terms, this doesn't make much sense, but teamwork often can't be quantified.

For example:

If you owned a chocolate factory who would you hire to work in it? Of course, you'd get yourself some loyal Oompa Loompas.

Let's say you asked these Oompa Loompas to make as many Everlasting Gobstoppers as they could in one hour. So, they went and began working in separate rooms. At the end of the hour, they each made one Everlasting Gobstopper.

In this scenario:

3 Oompa Loompas = 3 Gobstoppers

1 + 1+ 1 = 3

You're not too pleased with these results. You think the Oompa Loompas can do better. But maybe you didn't give them the proper instruction.

So, you give them one more hour to make as many Everlasting Gobstoppers as possible, but this time you ask them to work together, with each Oompa Loompa focusing on his or her personal strength.

This time, they sing their Oompa Loompa song and strategize about the best way to produce more Gobstoppers. They decide that one will focus on the molding, one will focus on the flavoring and coloring, and one will focus on the packaging. They now have a plan to maximize their individual efforts by working as a team.

Keep in mind, everything else is the same. There are still only three Oompa Loompas, and they still only have one hour, but the way they are working has changed.

By focusing on their strengths and working efficiently towards a common goal, the Oompa Loompas have a much better chance of making more Gobstoppers. If they each do their job then pass it to the next Oompa Loompa, there is a good chance these Oompa Loompas come back to you with 5 (or any number higher than the original 3) Everlasting Gobstoppers at the end of the hour.

In this scenario, because of *synergy*:

3 Oompa Loompas = 5 Gobstoppers

1+1+1=5

I'm no mathematician, but I've discovered putting teamwork into the equation yields huge results.

• • •

Anyone can work hard (and I strongly recommend that as well), but not everyone takes steps back to ask, "Can I work smarter?"

Take that step back every now and then.

Find *synergies* in your life that allow you to do great work in any area you choose. Young leaders consistently remind themselves that there's always room for improvement, and most often, failure is just another chance to learn.

Answer the Action Packed Discussion Questions and establish the areas in which you can work smarter then put your thoughts into action in your daily life!

*Chapter 7*

*Action Packed Discussion Questions*

*1. What types of Quadrant IV (not urgent and not important) activities are your kryptonite?*

*2. When have you worked well with others toward an end goal? What did you do that caused you to work well together?*

*3. How can you empower others to work hard to achieve a desired outcome?*

*4. How can you foster synergy in your classes? In your extracurricular organizations?*

Chapter 8 Preface

# MURPHY'S LAW

"How do you not get nervous when you speak in front of big groups?"

It is the number one question I get asked about the work I do as a speaker and leadership trainer across the country – and the truth is, I do get nervous.

There has never been a moment when I've been 100% comfortable going on stage. I care about what the audience thinks. I know this goes directly against all those people who say, "You shouldn't care what other people think." But the truth is that I do care. I want to do a good job. I want people in the crowd to think highly of me. I'm human, and these feelings are real.

It also makes me nervous to think about what could go wrong. Will I forget what I'm going to say? Will I trip and fall down? Will I accidentally say something I didn't mean?[62]

However, when you see me on stage, you wouldn't know all of this. I remember the first time I came to terms with the fact that all I could do was my best and hope that my audience enjoys it.

---

[62] By the way, I've now done all of those things – they're not as bad as you'd think.

My senior year of high school, I was the co-president of my high school DECA chapter.[63] My DECA partner and I decided we would compete in a category that allowed us to work on the project in advance (some categories are more spontaneous). We worked hard to prepare and practice our presentation and after doing well at the State Competition, we made it to the international competition in Atlanta, Georgia.

If you've heard the phrase, "If anything can go wrong, it will go wrong," then you may be able to guess how our trip to Atlanta went.

We had a four-hour drive to the airport; one mile into the trip we got a flat tire. After fixing the tire, we raced to the airport only to find that our flight had been delayed. After waiting for hours for our flight to leave, we were told that our flight had been cancelled.

At this point, everything was still fine. We would still arrive the next day in plenty of time to compete. I wasn't worried about it. But the bad luck wasn't over.

After spending the night near the airport, we got on our plane the next morning and flew to Atlanta. Upon arriving in Atlanta, we went to baggage claim and waited…and waited…and waited. Our luggage was lost.

Not only were our professional clothes not in Atlanta, all of our presentation materials had not arrived yet either. The woman at the airport assured us that they would be delivered to our hotel.

So, we went to our hotel, and I was excited to find out that there was a basketball court on the roof. We had a little bit of free time so I went up to play. It was great. There were a bunch of other people up there, and we played some intense games, but in the spirit of the trip, something bad was bound to happen. In my final game on the rooftop, I went up for a rebound, and as I did, caught a hard elbow straight to the face.

Now, I'm still of the philosophy that black eyes look pretty cool, but they don't look cool when you need to dress professionally and do a

---

[63] Along with a bright individual named Bre – Hi Bre!

presentation for judges. But there I was, sporting a nice big shiner on my eye.

Our materials came to the hotel in the nick of time, my DECA partner put make-up (yes, make-up) on my face to cover my black eye, and we went in to present to the judges.

I tell you all of this because there is rarely a time that everything goes your way and public speaking is no exception. I learned that day that I needed to be able to roll with the punches (literally). Although things prior to the presentation were not perfect by any means, we still walked in with confidence and did the best we could do.

I still remember the first line of our presentation, "Renowned author and radio host Tom Bodett once said, 'In school, you're taught a lesson and then given a test. In life, you're given a test that teaches you a lesson.'"

Ironically, I think this statement can be applied to what we went through on our trip to Atlanta. The lesson for me was that public speaking is all about confidence. All the things that happened prior to our presentation could have completely derailed us, but when the time to present came, we embraced it.

It worked out pretty well too as we placed in the top 20 in the world on our project. I still laugh wondering what the judges were thinking about my black eye that was still clearly visible despite the make-up.

This chapter is all about finding the confidence to use your voice.

I'll talk about:

- Finding your style
- The little things that make a big difference

Chapter 8
# PUBLIC SPEAKING

*"According to most studies, people's number one fear is public speaking. Number two is death. Death is number two. Does that sound right? This means to the average person, if you go to a funeral, you're better off in the casket than doing the eulogy."*

**Jerry Seinfeld**

Nothing you read can completely calm your public-speaking nerves – only practice can do that. Even then, you'll probably never feel completely comfortable – which I believe is a good thing – it means you care about your topic and hope it goes over well. I regularly speak to thousands of people as part of my job as a motivational speaker – and I *still* get nervous.

Even if you never have to get up on stage, overcoming your nerves to speak effectively is a vital skill. You need public speaking skills to make a class presentation, offer your input in a meeting, or make a sale. It'll make you a better communicator in general. Look at every opportunity to speak in public as an opportunity to develop your skills. This chapter will provide you with tips that will put you in a position to give a powerful presentation.

What we're really talking about here is finding your *voice*. While I've narrowed it down to *public speaking* – what I'm really talking about is finding the confidence to speak up, speak out, and embrace your role as an influencer in this world (because you are one).

When you believe your *voice can make a difference,* you then must begin the work of developing your style and speaking in the most authentic, and effective way.

## FIND YOUR STYLE

Are you loud or quiet? Funny or serious? Enthusiastic or composed? As a student leader, you must understand your personal style before speaking. An audience can pick out an inauthentic speaker right away. Find a style that fits your own personality, and you'll appear genuine. Remember, this must be more about *becoming* the best version of you than faking it.

To find your personal public speaking style, watch videos of great speakers. Look up politicians, stand-up comedians, or motivational speakers on YouTube for inspiration. Before deciding on the speaking style that fits you best, take notes and practice others' styles. Draw from them for inspiration, but still be authentic. Your speaking style should still be your own and flow from you naturally.

Try it out – head to YouTube and type in, "Great public speakers." Maybe try "Funny public speakers" next. Maybe try "Awesome speeches by high school students." See if you can find some videos to draw inspiration from.

Once you feel comfortable in your speaking style, there are a few more things to *think* clearly about. Below are the tried and true ways to absolutely nail whatever speech you are giving.

## DEVELOP

Preparation is necessary before delivering a speech. It is important to remember the speech sandwich when preparing your content:

Tell them what you're going to tell them.

Tell them.

Tell them what you told them.

This allows you to preview and review. You will give the audience an idea of what to expect and also provide a strong recap to close your presentation. Try to follow the speech sandwich model to develop an introduction, body, and conclusion. This allows the important messages to come through, and leaves out unnecessary fluff.

## AUDIENCE

Who you are speaking to makes a huge difference. Are you presenting to fellow students? Teachers? Parents? Is the setting formal or informal? While your presentation style should stay relatively consistent, your content, vocabulary, and jokes should be tailored to your audience. *Always* keep your audience in mind.

## DELIVER

Planning and preparation are only beneficial if you also have the confidence to deliver the message calmly and confidently. Things we've already discussed (eye contact, smiling, and nonverbal communication) apply to public speaking as well.

## TONE

This is the most important tool for influencing the emotional temperature of a room. Many students tighten up when giving a speech and try to do it "perfectly." There's no such thing as a perfect speech. What makes presentations interesting is that everyone has something different to say, and a different way to say it. Embrace what makes you unique and try speaking in front of crowds the same way you would speak to a friend.

I'm sure you've seen speakers who have instantly become robots the minute they stepped on stage. Trying to use a "presentation voice" removes authenticity from the presentation, appears awkward, and your audience will be more likely to zone out.

## POSTURE

Good posture indicates you're prepared to deliver your content. Poor posture displays a lack of confidence, uncertainty, or indifference. Look like you want to be there, even if you don't. Keep your shoulders back and your head up; this will set the stage for a strong presentation.

## HANDS

In *Talladega Nights*, Will Ferrell's character Ricky Bobby doesn't know what to do with his hands in an interview. He continues to unnaturally hold them up, while the reporter tries to coach him to put his hands back at his side.

To avoid looking like Ricky Bobby, use hand gestures *on purpose* when speaking in public. If using your hands feels unnatural, it's okay to leave your hands at your sides or folded in front of you.

Gesturing is used for emphasis. How much you gesture depends on the situation and your personal style of speaking. Someone like Jim Cramer, host of the TV show *Mad Money*, uses wild hand gestures to engage his audience. This works for him because he is a wild guy. More conservative speakers – politicians or professional speakers, for example – use milder hand gestures. The more you practice, the more natural your hand gestures will become.

Work to eliminate your nervous habits. Playing with your hair, hands, or any paper you might be holding is distracting. Especially when you are extremely nervous, this is challenging. All you can do is practice and try to calm your nerves.

## PACE

Moving too fast or too slow can ruin a presentation.

If no one can keep up because the speaker is moving too fast (like my college professor in the preface to Chapter 7), the audience won't know what the speaker is talking about.

If an audience gets bored by a presentation moving too slowly, they also won't know what the speaker is talking about…because they'll be asleep.

Find the pace that works for you and will resonate well with your audience. Work hard to keep the pace you've practiced during the actual presentation; many people tend to speed up when they're nervous. Take a breath and deliver the speech at the high level you know you're capable of.

## FILLERS

QUOTABLE:

Filler words are usually used to remove pauses or dead space during a speech. But this dead space is often just what you need to make a speech impactful! Pauses allow the audience to absorb what you're saying. As Claude Debussy once said, "Music is the space between the notes."

*"Music is the space between the notes."*

–CLAUDE DEBUSSY

Fillers detract from your credibility. I used to keep a tally of how many times my high school physics teacher said "mmkay?" in one class period. It was so distracting! Everyone noticed. Some filler words – "like" for example – have become a part of our everyday speech. You didn't *like* go to the movies – you *went* to the movies – no likes about it. Especially when we're nervous, we speak quickly and overuse fillers. If you catch yourself doing this during a speech, take a deep breath, remind yourself to speak slowly, and pause frequently.

## FEET

Movement during a speech is a positive thing (unless you're behind a podium, then it isn't recommended). But students often anxiously sway, shift their feet, and walk aimlessly without even realizing it. These nervous movements are distracting and detract from your message. Next time you make a presentation, have someone film you. This is a great way to see movement that might otherwise fly under the radar.

*Positive* movements have a purpose. For example, acting out something you're explaining in your speech can keep the audience engaged. If your story involves running, you could act out a jog as you speak.

---

*"When I was preparing for my first speaking competition in seventh grade, I began seeing an acting coach. This was not to make my performance more dramatic, but to work on my awkward, seventh-grade stage presence. My coach taught me that body language is almost formulaic: a comfortable bend of the knees reveals an easy-goingness; light gestures in a business environment show professionalism and engagement; a turn of feet out slightly in a V underneath the shoulders can prevent nervous rocking. My coach's advice still runs through my mind as I prepare to give presentations, whether it is for 10 or 100 people. Non-verbal communication is a piece of the puzzle to unlocking the professional inside all students. We can speak eloquently and look charming – but sometimes the difference between a great communicator and one with less polish is what we do with our bodies, not our words."*

—Rachel Wagner
Former Delaware Business Professionals of America (BPA)
National Officer

---

## PRACTICE

As with anything, the only way to improve your speaking skills is to practice. As Maya Angelou so profoundly said: "Ain't nothin' to it, but to do it." Put yourself out there! Volunteer to speak even when you're nervous or uncertain. Stepping up to use your *voice* is initially awkward for everyone. Remind yourself that public speaking abilities are not developed overnight. Do your best to face your fear of speaking in public, and practice often.

...

Speaking in front of others is difficult, even for the best of young leaders. Use the tips in this chapter to give you the edge you need to get in front of a group and nail it.

It takes courage to put yourself out there, *but the more you go outside of your comfort zone the larger your comfort zone becomes.* Work to find your speaking style then hone your skills by mastering the little things and soon you'll find it easier to use your *voice* and rise to any occasion that calls to you.

## CHAPTER 8 ACTION PACKED DISCUSSION QUESTIONS

*1. Whose speaking style do you like most? How can you emulate their style in your own speaking?*

*2. What are your go-to filler words?*

*3. What are the symptoms of your speaking anxiety? How can you work to overcome them?*

*4. What do you do with your hands and feet when you speak? How can you make your movements more natural and effective?*

Chapter 9 Preface

# STARTING SOMEWHERE

At the time of writing this book I've spoken in 47 states.[64]

My full-time job is to travel the country and deliver messages on positivity, kindness, and action. I'd like to think I've gotten a lot better at speaking over the years, and I'm certain I'll continue to get better as I go.

But before I was ever trusted to give my first professional speech, I was an intern just like so many young college students.

As a sophomore in college, I became an intern at a leadership development company in Milwaukee, Wisconsin. They specialized in providing youth leadership training to groups around the country, but at the time of my interviews they weren't looking for speakers; they were in need of a sales intern.

My responsibilities as an intern consisted of making phone calls and having sales-oriented conversations with high school principals around the country. In all honesty, I didn't love it. It wasn't the best fit for me,

---

[64] I still need to check off Hawaii, Rhode Island, and West Virginia.

but I did love the company and saw potential for other opportunities that might be a better fit.

I began asking if I could get involved in the speaking and leadership training side of the business. I still laugh thinking about me as a sophomore in college asking if I could become a speaker for students a year or two younger than me.

It wasn't much of a surprise that the company didn't drop everything and realize I was the next big thing, but they did give me a shot.

At the first program I ever spoke I was given 5 minutes to discuss goal-setting. I remember sweating profusely as I tried to hide my nerves. I was handed the microphone and away I went.

I can't remember what I said or if it went over well, but it must not have been a complete train wreck because small opportunities for me to speak continued to pop up after that day.

Both my abilities as a speaker and my opportunities to use them grew throughout my time in college, and the company that gave me my first chance as an intern ended up bringing me on as a full-time speaker after I graduated from college. They even agreed to publish my first book!

Since then I've started my own leadership development company, Action Packed Leadership, published two more books (you're currently holding one of them), and continue to grow every day.

Everyone needs to start somewhere.

For me, my speaking career started by making phone calls to high school principals.

It would have been easy at the time to get frustrated and say, "I know I could be a speaker; it's stupid no one is giving me a chance." But that's not how trust works. I couldn't earn it overnight, and I'm sure you can't either. I spent over two years as an intern at a leadership development company before I was able to make public speaking my profession.

*Trust* is an understated quality in a leader. As always, a quality like *trust* begins with how we *think*. Our internalized values will come through in our actions over time – these actions, based on how we think, will indicate to others whether we are trustworthy or not.

Building and enhancing the trust of others is essential for any student leader.

In this chapter I'll discuss how our *thoughts* turned to *actions* develop trust. Specifically, I'll cover:

- Consistency and time
- Communication
- The value of a shared vision
- Vulnerability

Chapter 9
# BUILDING TRUST

*"Trust is the glue of life. It's the most essential ingredient in effective communication. It's the foundational principle that holds all relationships."*

—**Stephen Covey**

Mutual trust is necessary to maintain close personal relationships – I'm sure you already know this. If you don't trust someone or he or she doesn't trust you, the odds you'll remain close to this person is low.

But trust should extend far beyond your relationships with friends, family, or a significant other. Student leaders cultivate trust *on purpose* in all group settings to ensure work is shared, responsibilities are managed, and deadlines are met.

Obtaining the *status* of a leader does not automatically yield trust.

If you become the president of your Student Council, great! But this doesn't automatically mean your peers need to trust you. True leaders must *earn* trust and reinforce through daily actions *why* they deserve it.

When young people expect trust before they earn it the world calls them *entitled*.

Even with the best intentions, skills, and ideas your legacy as a leader cannot be complete without trust which is why we need to begin, like always, with how we *think* about it.

The first and most important brain swap we need to do is to take trust from the bottom to the top of our priority list. We need to understand every chapter before this one can help us earn trust, but trust is a deeper quality that isn't a one-time or a scenario-driven action.

Trust is made up of every interaction you have with someone else. It is gained or lost with every word you say.

In this way, trust is *strategic* when most of the other qualities are *tactical*.

*Tactical* qualities are like music notes. If you read the notes correctly and play them at the proper times, you'll complete the musical piece flawlessly.

*Strategic* qualities are like choosing which musical pieces go together perfectly to give an audience a great experience. There is a lot of nuance to it, and it isn't as simple as just following instructions.

*Tactics* are step-by-step actions. *Strategies* are well-crafted plans.

This is why I've saved the chapter on trust for later in this book. There is more nuance to building trust than just simple actions you can take here or there.

Allow everything you've read up until this point contribute to your understanding of how to build trust through positive and intentional thought.

Both professionally and personally, trust is the foundation of success. Like networking, gaining and then maintaining the trust of others is a continuous and conscious process.

In this chapter, I'll give you ways that I know to build and grow trust as a young leader.

## CONSISTENCY AND TIME

Trust is like a Persian rug.

Persian rugs can take years, sometimes even lifetimes, to create. All of the stitching is done by hand, and one small error could harm the entire rug. Trust takes time, and it is much easier lost than built.

I'll say that again: *trust is much easier lost than built*[65].

**FYI** — Depending on its fineness, a Persian rug can have between 16 and 800 knots per square inch.

I'm sure you can think of an example in your own life of a time when the trust you had in someone else was all lost in an instant.

Building trust doesn't happen overnight, but it most certainly can be lost overnight.

*The best way to gain trust is to act with integrity.*

*Integrity* is simply *being honest* and having strong *moral values*.

*Integrity* is built up over *real time* experiences.

Others will associate the word integrity with your *personal brand* when you demonstrate your moral values over time – not just once, but consistently.

At a basic level, it is what you *do* that will define you, and as you've learned, your *thoughts* will direct these *actions*.

From an *integrity* standpoint, when we push our thoughts to include *fairness, truth,* and *justice* we'll be much more apt to include these qualities in our day-to-day *actions*.

From strictly an *action* standpoint, don't do anything that might diminish others' trust in you – *cheating, lying,* or *gossiping* – for example.

---

[65] Like getting six-pack abs.

By choosing to *act* with *integrity*, you are taking a strong stance on what qualities will make up your *character*.

Do your work honestly and responsibly.

Complete assignments and manage responsibilities, especially when others depend on you.

*Be nice.*

Consistently acting with *integrity* will build trust with others better than any leadership title.

In this poem by an unknown author, the concept of trust is paralleled with the slow and careful process of building:

> *I saw them tearing a building down*
> *A team of men in my hometown.*
> *With a heave and a ho and a yes yes yell,*
> *They swung a beam and a sidewall fell.*
>
> *And I said to the foreman, "Are these men skilled?"*
> *"Like the ones you'd use if you had to build?"*
> *And he laughed and said, "Oh no, indeed...*
> *The most common labor is all I need...*
> *For I can destroy in a day or two*
> *What takes a builder years to do."*
>
> *So I thought to myself as I went on my way...*
> *Which one of these roles am I willing to play?*
> *Am I one who is tearing down as I carelessly make my way around?*
> *Or am I one who builds with care, to make the world better...*
> *because I was there?*

## COMMUNICATE

Picture for a moment your best friend asks you to go somewhere with them:

> You: "Where are we going?"
> Friend: "I'm not going to tell you; just come with me."

Would you go?

Of course, you would! It's your best friend! If you *wouldn't* go, you might want to consider how trustworthy your friends are.

Now imagine a complete stranger asks you to go somewhere with them.

> You: "Where are we going?"
> Stranger: "I'm not going to tell you; just come with me."

Would you go?

I certainly hope not. Actually, you should probably call the police.

Now imagine a student in your school said these same things to you. Someone with whom you are familiar, but are not close friends.

Would you go?

**QUOTABLE:**

*"Stand for what you believe in, even if it means standing alone.."*

—ANDY BIERSACK

Your response might depend on your personality, but most students would ask more questions and be at least somewhat skeptical. In your mind, you'll most likely have questions like, "Will this be fun? Who else will be there? What am I going to have to do? Etc."

In the end, what you're really trying to figure out is, "Can I trust this person?"

This is simply an example of the trust built through *time* and *communication*.

Your best friend has (hopefully) communicated his or her trustworthiness over time. A complete stranger? Not so much. This person may very well be extremely trustworthy, but it hasn't been communicated *to you* in any way. The acquaintance at school? You'll most likely think about your experiences with this person before making a decision one way or the other.

Long story short, trust is built over *time* by *communicating* values effectively.

Within a team, *communicating expectations,* just like getting informed of where you're going by your best friend, is an appropriate way to ensure everyone is moving in the same direction. When expectations are set, teams then must learn to trust that each member of the team is working toward the common goal.

Knowing the monetary goal of a fundraiser or the expected grade for a group project will put everyone on the same page.

By defining where you are going, you give others an opportunity to come along. When they do, they bring new skills and perspectives to help young leaders get to the goal they've communicated.

## FOCUS ON SHARED GOALS

Not everything is about you – at least it shouldn't be. To truly build trust, treat everyone you work with as equals, and be inclusive. As someone close to me once said, "I would rather be excluded because of who I include, than included because of who I exclude." Include every member of your team when building shared goals – people support what they help to create.

Goals should reflect the desires of the team, and not just the leader.

Shared goals allow everyone to become invested in the project. Ask for feedback often to make sure everyone is invested in the process.

This. Is. Important.

Most young people miss this part. It is great to have shared goals amongst a team, but trust is truly built during the *process* of completing goals. Within the process, check in with your team. Discuss what is going well. Offer help if someone has hit a road bump.

You'll find you earn a lot more trust when you are *consistent* in your *availability* to others when they need you.

## OPEN UP

Too often, the most driven students feel the need to succeed in everything. Expecting perfection of yourself is wearing and disappointing.

You're *not* perfect, and no one expects you to be.

Ask for help and split responsibilities when you need to. Vulnerability does not harm your credibility as a student leader. In fact, your honesty and communication will provide a greater foundation for trust, and can reduce your workload.

There are lots of ways to *show* vulnerability, but for now, just focus on the way you *think* about vulnerability.

Do you think it is valuable to be open and honest with others or a waste of time?

Do you think being real with team members will lead them to trusting you more?

Do you think your personal story has value?

My hope is that you do believe your story has value – I personally believe everyone's story has value. Unfortunately, not everyone believes this. Maybe right now is your moment to change your mind.

If you're looking for the tactical ways to show vulnerability as a way to build trust, below are a few examples.

Share a personal story or something embarrassing that once happened to you.

Share about your failures and mistakes so others can learn from them.

Share a time when you doubted yourself and ended up succeeding.

When others see you being vulnerable, they are more likely to relate to what you've been through which typically leads to more trust.

While it is important to be vulnerable, it is also important not to be reckless.

You don't need to open up to people who aren't trustworthy or you feel will be harmful emotionally to you.

## ASK FOR HELP RESPONSIBLY

Asking for help is a *good thing*.

Just about every teacher I've ever spoken with would rather have a student ask them for help than have a student not turn in an assignment.

However, when you ask for help, do so responsibly.

Plan ahead, and don't wait until the last minute when a deadline is urgent and expect others to jump to your aid.

An appropriate and responsible way to ask for help may be to say something like, "Hey Laura, we have a few deadlines coming up in the next two weeks, and I think I might need some help from you to be able to hit them. I can give you more details, but is this something you might be able to spend some time with me on? Can we talk tonight?"

This saves the other person from feeling anxious because you've burdened them with a last-minute task.

Similarly, as we had talked about when discussing character, be sure to return the favor when someone needs your help if you are capable.

Trust is difficult to build, and easy to tear down.

Begin cultivating trust with everyone: teammates, coworkers, classmates, teachers, parents, and fellow leaders.

Keep in mind that trust is a *strategic* quality meaning you'll have to use all the other leadership skills in this book to figure out how to *act* trustworthy.

The goal of trust is to create relationships that benefit everyone involved – it is never to *get* something from someone else; this would be a pretty untrustworthy thing to do.

By consistently *acting with integrity*, being *open and vulnerable*, and asking for *help* when you need it you'll have your start to building trust with everyone you meet. And these trusting relationships will benefit you for years to come.

## CHAPTER 9 ACTION PACKED DISCUSSION QUESTIONS

*1. In which of your relationships is there a high level of trust? How was it built?*

*2. How can you build trust in relationships on purpose – with people other than your family and closest friends?*

*3. How can you cultivate trust as a leader? As a follower?*

*4. How can you help others and get others to help you?*

Chapter 10 Preface
# LIFE IS A MARATHON

I'm sure you've heard the phrase, "Life is not a sprint. It's a marathon."

When I was in high school and even most of college I had no idea what this meant.

My life was consistently made up of short-term items that I needed to check off a list. Do this assignment. Check. Study for this test. Check. Go to practice. Check. The longest I really had to focus on anything during those periods of my life was a semester. No teachers ever said, "Okay, this project is due in two years." That would have made my brain explode.

This is until my college roommate, Kevin, encouraged me to run an actual marathon. No metaphors. No "marathon of life" stuff. Just a good old-fashioned 26.2-mile run.

I found out pretty quickly why people say life is a marathon. The training itself takes forever. I mean forever. It feels like every day is another long run, and it lasts for months.

The marathon I had signed up for was scheduled for July in Madison, Wisconsin.

I changed my diet. I ran a crazy number of hours on weekends. I put everything I had into being ready for this race.

When the day of the race came, I woke up ready to run. Finally, all my hard work was going to pay off. I was excited to get to the starting line (and even more excited to get to the finish line).

However, the morning of the race, I ran[66] into an unexpected issue.

The race coordinators decided to cancel the marathon because they felt the heat index was too dangerous to run 26.2 miles.

"Excuse me??"

I went from shock, to anger, to extreme disappointment.

I mean I was devastated.

I had put in so much work. I had spent early mornings running for hours before class started. I had even started spending money on fruit! What sane college student does that?

All my time and effort felt like it was wasted, and I started getting bitter about the whole situation thinking I would never even attempt to run another marathon.

Even worse, my cancelled marathon affected my energy in other areas of my life. I felt cheated. Something I wanted to do so badly was taken from me and it was out of my control. My motivation to do good work fell, and I had a hard time getting out of bed in the morning.

Then I realized something – maybe THAT marathon was out of my control, but everything else since that day was completely IN my control.

I changed my attitude immediately and stopped feeling sorry for myself.

I realized how incredible it is that my muscles work, and I was in the physical shape to run a marathon.

It took me over a year after my cancelled race, but I finally decided I was going to finish a marathon – not because I NEEDED to finish a marathon,

---

[66] Not literally

but because I had a goal and fell short, and I still had the opportunity to complete that goal.

My training started up again and was easier this time around because I now had a chip on my shoulder; I wouldn't skip workouts or take shortcuts because I was 100 percent resolved to run this marathon.

I even thought to myself, "They cancelled my marathon in Wisconsin. I'm going to run a cooler one."

I went online and Googled, "Coolest Marathons."

This story does have a happy ending.

Because my marathon was cancelled and I resolved to run a cooler one, I ended up flying across the world and running the *original marathon* from Marathon to Athens, Greece in the Fall of 2013!

It was an amazing experience to travel all that way and complete a goal I had set nearly two years prior. It took a lot of resilience, patience, and positive energy, but I did it, and to this day it is one of my proudest moments.

Since my first marathon in 2013, I've run five other marathons (in Louisiana, Oregon, Singapore, North Carolina, and Michigan).

While running a marathon itself is difficult, the build-up and training for each marathon is even more challenging, and the barriers I overcame to complete my first marathon taught me a lot about what it takes to stay motivated over a long period of time.

Life is the same way.

It doesn't fit into semesters, and long-term goals take persistence and work. They take resilience, patience, and a lot of positive energy, and sometimes the barriers we're forced to overcome are just pushing us to something bigger and better.

This chapter is all about staying motivated. We'll discuss:

- Your friends
- Escaping boredom
- Actionable ways to stay motivated

Chapter 10
# STAYING MOTIVATED

"*Start where you are. Use what you have. Do what you can.*"

—Arthur Ashe

Young leaders have a reputation for trying to have everything together – because more than most students, they do. But *no one* has it all figured out. We all need help at times.

You are human and you are young, don't expect yourself to be a superhero. You don't have to be a productive, positive, go-getter at all times. Take a moment to recognize when you need rest and take care of yourself before you get sick, experience burnout, or become overwhelmed.

Like everyone else, young leaders get stuck in ruts of laziness and procrastination. It happens to the best of us.

Staying motivated isn't easy.

When you need to practice self-care, please do it. However, sometimes you need a figurative kick in the pants to get yourself moving again.

So where can this motivation come from?

## YOU ARE WHO YOU HANG OUT WITH

In the same way practicing with great athletes will make you a better athlete yourself, surrounding yourself with other leaders will motivate and encourage you on a regular basis to be the best leader you can be.

Spending time with the right people is absolutely vital to the success of a young leader.

If all of your friends play video games instead of working on an assignment, it's easier to put the assignment off and start gaming with them.

If your friends start drinking alcohol or experimenting with different illegal substances, your chances of doing these same things go up.

When I was a junior in high school, an 8th grade girl I had met only a couple times sent me a message online telling me she was scared to get to high school. She asked me if I had any advice.

I remember telling her to be careful choosing friends and to make sure she stands firm in what she believes. I told her to be ready to say no if asked to participate in things she doesn't want to do.

I'm ashamed to say I lost track of her for quite some time when she got to high school. I didn't follow up with her or ask her how it was going. I didn't help her find friends or navigate the hallways. I still feel bad about not being there for her after she had reached out to me for my help. If I could go back, I would do things very differently.

I came to find out after I graduated from high school she was spending most of her time with people I knew to be heavy drinkers and partiers. She seemed to have gone down the exact path she was afraid of. The friends she surrounded herself with when she got to high school were not helping her become a better version of herself. They were leading her in the exact direction she didn't want to go.

Who are your friends?

Are they making you better or making you worse?

What I'm absolutely not telling you is that you need to drop your friends just because they like Fortnite.

Friends are always a little "distracting" – they're there to have fun and relax with you.

But aligning yourself with people who share your *mindset* and *values* makes it easier to stay motivated.

You won't feel like you're missing out on a great video game session if your friends are working on their assignments as well.

And of course, you want to have friends who build you up and want to see you succeed. If you choose not to attend parties because of your involvement in a sport, this type of friend will understand.

## DON'T BE BORING

We all experience moments of feeling unmotivated.

Below are some *tactical* tips for staying motivated and keeping your life and work interesting:

- Work hard. Student leaders work harder than their peers and know their hard work is going to pay off. As Vince Lombardi said, "The only place success comes before work is in the dictionary." Knowing the work they do is meaningful keeps young leaders energized.
- Get creative with your day-to-day activities. It is easy for students to say, "I'm bored because there is nothing to do in my town." There are a million things you could do if you take a more creative approach. Don't believe me? Type, "Things to do in a small town," into Google. You'll find hundreds of suggestions. Try one. Try ten. Don't let yourself fall victim to *boredom thinking*.
- Add this creativity to work time. This will make your work much more enjoyable and interesting. Go to a new place to study, set up some sort of competition (whoever completes these math problems first wins), or do something outside of the box for an

assignment. A PowerPoint does not have to be boring; it could also include screenshots of relevant social media posts to spice it up and drive home relevant points. Getting creative with presentations and assignments will be refreshing for both you and your teachers.

» Stay positive. The power of positive thinking is vital. Someone once told me that people who smile because they want other people to think they are happy actually become *less* happy. People who choose to smile based on their own thoughts rather than the perceptions of others become happier over time. Decide you're going to be happy for yourself. *Your thoughts matter.*

## MOTIVATION HACKS

Below are some life hacks to keep you motivated. These are *specific actions* you can take that may help – don't forget to keep in mind the *thoughts* behind these actions as they are the true drivers of everything you do.

» *212* Set an alarm on your phone every day for 2:12 in the afternoon. Why 2:12? At 211 degrees Fahrenheit, water is hot. At 212 degrees, water boils. And the steam from boiling water can generate enough energy and electricity to fuel a locomotive. 2:12 PM can be your daily reminder to go that extra degree in whatever you are working on, knowing that big things can happen because of it.

» *Eating and Exercise* Eating right can improve energy levels and keep you at the top of your game – fruits and vegetables go a long way. Similarly, doing something physical is stress-relieving. Take up yoga, take the dog for a walk, or have a dance party in your bedroom. Do something physical when you feel stressed. You'll have more energy to get things done and have more fun along the way.

» *Motivate Others* By making it your responsibility to motivate those around you, it will be much easier to keep yourself motivated. Think to yourself, "What type of leadership do the people around me need?" and work to be the person to bring that energy to them.

- ***Make Goals Visible*** Have your goals written and visible. They'll stay on your mind if you can look at them every day. Write them on a mirror or keep them on your phone. By keeping your goals in sight, you are less likely to forget about them or lose focus over time.
- ***Smaller Tasks*** Break large projects up into smaller tasks and complete them one by one. Have checkpoints along the way and reward yourself for progress made.
- ***Make Your Bed*** Making your bed when you first wake up will set the stage to accomplish tasks for the rest of the day. It will make you feel organized and lead to a more productive day right from the start.
- ***You Don't Always Need to Smile*** Famous entrepreneur and author, Gary Vaynerchuk (the man I met through my AJ Bombers experience), will tell you to focus first on the things that make you frown. This seems a little depressing, but his point is to encourage people to see the big picture. Do the hard work now, and you'll be happier in the future. It's much more fulfilling to become successful when you know you have put blood, sweat, and tears into a project. You won't be smiling while putting in the necessary work, but it will lead to a much brighter smile when you've accomplished the goals you set out to accomplish. Frown now; smile later.

. . .

Leaders are human and have lapses in motivation – it happens. We all need breaks to refresh our minds (remember the Brain Breaks section earlier in this book).

However, an overall feeling of increased motivation, like other skills in this book, can be *conditioned*. The more you're able to practice your motivational endurance, the better you'll be able to consistently bring your energy to the table.

Those who push themselves to work hard, focus well, and accomplish big things will find it easier to do so every day. Come back to this chapter from time to time if you feel yourself slipping into patterns of procrastination. There are plenty of helpful hints you could put into *action* to give yourself the motivational boost you're looking for.

---

*"The habits you develop in high school won't evaporate when that diploma is handed to you. Working hard to accomplish things is an ability that must be developed, and high school and college are awesome opportunities to develop those skills."*

—Matt Sabljak
President of SRH Marketing
(He wrote this when he was one year out of high school)

---

## CHAPTER 10 ACTION PACKED DISCUSSION QUESTIONS

1. Do the people you spend time with want to see you succeed?

2. Which of the "Motivation Hacks" can you employ to keep yourself motivated?

3. What is one project or goal that you have been highly motivated to complete? How have you been able to stay focused?

4. What causes you to lose motivation? How can you reduce the time you spend on this activity?

Chapter 11 Preface

# YOU'RE FIRED

The summer after my sophomore year in college I had a part-time internship with a technology startup in Milwaukee, Wisconsin.

I learned so much from this internship experience working with some of the most talented people I've ever met.

My boss, Matt, was a 25-year-old fireball of a sales manager who was quick-witted and extremely bright[67]. Through the course of my internship, we worked together on quite a few projects and had a lot of fun in the process. We tackled tasks with so much energy, it was hard not to enjoy our work.

As I neared the end of my internship, Matt asked if I wanted to be on his weekly basketball team.

No one in high school ever told me you could have fun outside of work with your boss. In the business community, this is 100% true.

I excitedly accepted the invitation to play on his team.

---

[67] You may remember him as one of my interviewers from earlier who told me to start a Twitter account and talked about fruit-shaped soap.

Skip ahead 5 years.

I was traveling the country speaking with the leadership development company that hired me after college, and I was still playing basketball with Matt as much as I could.

Matt and I would meet up on weekends to talk about our business aspirations and work on projects together. When my first book was published, Matt even said a few words at my book launch party.

In 2015, Matt decided to start his own business with two partners – they named it SRH Marketing.

We were working together at a coffee shop one weekend when he said, "Kyle, I'm going to hire you."

I laughed at first and said, "Don't you think I should have a say in this?"

We both thought it was pretty funny, but he continued to think about how he could bring me onto the team at SRH.

Sure enough, 5 months later he extended an offer I couldn't turn down, and I became his first employee.

In the coming months, we had built a million-dollar business! I couldn't believe it; I started to picture my future with this company – earning tons of money and working alongside a good friend.

However, not all stories have a stereotypical "happy ending." Sometimes the silver linings are harder to see.

I started to realize my passions were not in my work at SRH, and I lost a lot of motivation and focus. Matt started to see my lack of energy and questioned whether I wanted to be working there at all.

Even during times of business growth, I was having trouble finding my footing in my role and found myself shutting down more and more under the stress and pressure of building a marketing firm from the ground up.

I started writing my second book to take my mind off the pressure, which began taking more and more of my time away from the work I was supposed to be doing at SRH.

After 9 months at SRH, the two of us sat down alongside another partner of the firm and Matt said those fateful words, "We don't think this is working out. We're going to have to let you go."

I was fired that day.

It was embarrassing and difficult, and filled me with anxiety. I held back tears as we discussed all the specifics, then I went to pack up my things.

As I finished packing everything up, Matt came over and gave me a hug.

I'm sure neither of us saw our business relationship going down this way.

It took me a while to realize that Matt was trying to do what was best for both the company and for me. He knew my passions were elsewhere, and he wanted to give me an opportunity to pursue them.

As hard as that day was, I look back and think I wouldn't be where I am today – sharing stories around the country as the founder of my own leadership development company – if it wasn't for Matt.

We still keep in touch, which I think is pretty wild. How many people still keep in touch with the person who fired them? Matt has even recommended me to speak for school programs he's come across.

Although I've moved out of Milwaukee, it was clear the invitation to be a part of his basketball team was more than just playing basketball. It was about looking out for each other and maintaining a positive relationship even in the midst of unfortunate circumstances.

Through the course of your lifetime you will gain friends, lose friends, build relationships, and burn bridges. There will be a constant ebb and flow of people in and out of your life.

This chapter is all about maintaining meaningful relationships.

Networking can be a great asset (as you've already learned), but if all your connections are just people you met once, they most likely won't be very helpful to you. Building strong relationships that last is a powerful leadership tool that will benefit you for the rest of your life.

In this chapter, I'll talk about:

- Thoughtfulness
- Being random
- Interacting with a purpose
- Building equity
- Generosity

Chapter 11
# MAINTAINING RELATIONSHIPS

*"Nothing is perfect. Life is messy. Relationships are complex. Outcomes are uncertain. People are irrational."*

—Hugh Mackay

Healthy relationships are a vital component of our well-being.

They are also vital to our personal and professional successes. This chapter expands on what we discussed in the Networking portion of the book. You've learned how to create a *connection*, but how do you keep one? Long-term connections are not easy to establish, but they are well worth it.

Before we get going, let's do a quick check-in.

We know relationships with others begin with our own *thoughts*.

We understand our *thoughts* will naturally become our *actions*.

When we've established, through positive *thought*, our *integrity* by intentionally building our *values*, we are able to maintain more genuine *relationships* over longer periods of time.

And we know the best relationships are ones that benefit everyone involved equally.

There is no telling what type of benefit a connection can have for you in the future – or what benefit you can bring to a future connection. Young leaders recognize connections can come in handy in many ways, and most of these ways are unseen at the time of meeting.

Below is your guide to think like a leader when it comes to maintaining relationships.

## BE THOUGHTFUL

Have you ever heard the saying, "It's the thought that counts?"

Thoughtfulness isn't a simple action that happens once and is then done.

Thoughtfulness means you are putting time and energy into thinking about how you can add value to the life of someone else.

When we think of being thoughtful, sometimes we gravitate to the boyfriend who buys his girlfriend flowers. "You are so thoughtful!"

But there are plenty of ways to be thoughtful without being romantic, and you can utilize some of these in your business and personal relationships.

Go out of your way to maintain contact with people and let them know you appreciate them.

Send a thank-you note to a teacher who wrote you a letter of recommendation.

E-mail members of your club about progress you're making, and thank them for their work.

Send a Facebook message to a friend to see how they're doing.

Simple things like remembering a birthday shows that you care and goes a long way.

Do you want to really blow someone's mind? The next time they tell you about something important, set a reminder in your phone to ask them about it the next day. If they have a piano recital coming up, the day after it happens, send them a text asking how it was. It doesn't take a lot of time, but it will show them you were really listening and care about them as a person.

Student leaders think of others, even when it is not easy to do so. They understand that they cannot accomplish anything alone, and that maintaining healthy relationships can help them get fundraiser donations, acceptance letters, scholarships, new jobs, fresh perspectives, and career advice. Heck, good relationships with classmates may get a young person voted Prom King or Queen.

However, as you've learned in this book, it is not simply the thought that counts. It is your thought turned to action that makes all the difference.

## BE RANDOM

By this, I don't mean to just say crazy things out of the blue.

That would probably be the opposite of good advice. Can you imagine? You're just sitting in class and out of nowhere yell, "Carrots are my favorite vegetable!" Your teacher would not be too pleased.

What I mean is to not fret if you haven't talked to someone in a while. It's okay to reach back out to them, even if it is unexpected or may appear random.

Don't be afraid to get in touch with old connections. Remind them when you met each other if you think it is needed.

Contact someone you have lost touch with. A "random" text can be a pleasant surprise and serve as a reminder that you still value your relationship with them. Bonus points if this random text includes something nice about them or something you miss because you haven't talked in a while.

For some of you, I'm sure I'm preaching to the choir. For others, you may never do any of these things. My simple hope is that you would think about the relationships you value, and take action to show it.

Don't be afraid to randomly reach out to people outside of your circle of friends. As I mentioned in the Networking chapter, not all relationships have the same purpose or level of intimacy. Connect with people outside of your friend circle. "Random" relationships can offer you fresh perspectives. The more positive relationships in your life, the better.

You may even want to reach out randomly to some famous people online asking for tips, tricks, or advice. One of the times I did this, billionaire entrepreneur Mark Cuban shared some great advice with me.

When you think about creating and maintaining relationships, it is more than okay to be random at times; embrace the unknown and reach out. You never know what could come from it.

*"Many times people say, "It is not what you know, but who you know." This statement is partially true (it's what you know, too). It's vital to learn how to create relationships that are mutually beneficial and based on trust. Do not dismiss a relationship just because you are not getting much out of it – they shouldn't be based on personal gain. In my experience, the relationships in which you give as much as you receive are the most rewarding."*

—Katie Brown
Former Wisconsin DECA Vice President of Business Partnerships

## BE PURPOSEFUL

It takes effort to maintain relationships.

Approach relationships *purposefully*.

Consciously reconnect with people to keep from drifting apart.

It should be pretty clear from everything you've previously read that gaining a job, a leadership position, or money are not the only outcomes that can come from maintaining positive professional relationships. Some of the most meaningful relationships you'll ever have are about the experience – the *learning* you obtain because of the relationship.

Learn from the experiences of every one of your connections.

The more connections you have, the more experiences you have to draw from. In writing this book, I was able to reach out to old friends, co-workers, and acquaintances for their thoughts, criticism, and advice. I reached out to people on social media along with State Officers of student organizations, presidents of Student Councils, Eagle Scouts, and every young person who approached me after one of my talks. Their input and support provided the necessary information and content for this book to be created. This assistance was incredibly valuable to me – I was able to use the experience of others to bring my thoughts full-circle. You can also do this with everyone you meet.

Recall from the Networking chapter: maintaining relationships is not about *using* others for personal benefit. In the example above, I sincerely hope I have provided equal or more value to every one of those connections. It may not always be the case, but it was never my intent to *use* anyone simply for my personal gain.

Connections should not be forced, or approached with an end goal in mind. I didn't develop relationships with old friends and co-workers hoping to one day use them for input in my book. Our relationships are genuine, mutually beneficial, and based on respect. When you approach your relationships with purpose, these are the relationships that will ensue.

## BUILD EQUITY

Students are often reluctant to ask for help for fear of appearing needy or unprepared. When help is available, it's okay to take it. Don't waste time feeling lost or stressed. Reaching out is a good thing – it reaffirms your relationship. As author and CEO Keith Ferrazzi will tell you,

"It's the exercising of equity that builds equity." This simply means when there is more contact, communication, and honesty between individuals, the more equity (or value) is built, and the stronger their relationship will become. When you wait and wait and wait to get in touch with someone after meeting them, they'll most likely have forgotten you when you finally do reach out.

> **QUOTABLE**
>
> *"It's the exercising of equity that builds equity"*
>
> —KEITH FERRAZZI

Ask your connections for help. Seek advice and wisdom from more experienced people you know. Don't hold back. If someone says no to helping, do your best to not take it personally and move on to someone who may be willing to assist.

And in the spirit of *thinking* like a leader and allowing your actions to follow – if you *know* you are working to build mutually beneficial relationships, there will be work you'll want to *do*. When others ask you for advice, time, or work, do your best to help them knowing that this always lays the foundation for a better relationship in the future.

## BE GENEROUS

The real secret of networking and maintaining relationships is not what others can give you, but what you can provide others.

In an interview on *The Chris Farley Show*, Paul McCartney said, "The more you give, the more you get." This may have been a comedy sketch on Saturday Night Live, but the sentiment rings true.

Young leaders benefit from serving others.

Doing good for others should *not* stem from the expectation that you'll benefit in the future. Be generous for no reason other than you as a student leader enjoy helping those around you and be *grateful* for any benefits you may get in return for your service.

Be sure to also recognize the different ways you can grow from a relationship.

As a math tutor, you can likely provide more help than those you are tutoring can provide for you. The scales may not be exactly even on who is benefiting more. But you can gain experience, friendship, patience, or satisfaction from a job well done because of your tutoring experience. You may even be able to point to your experience as a tutor on an application or in an interview. Tutor because it's the right thing to do, and recognize the indirect ways that doing good helps you grow.

If you're the one receiving the help, show your appreciation however you can. Gratitude can go a long, long way.

. . .

Almost everything we can ever *accomplish* or *become* is going to be the result of *help from others*.

To receive this help, we have to build and maintain the right type of relationships every day.

Add water to the seeds of your relationships whenever possible.

All great leaders work to make great connections. Use the tips in this chapter to maintain those relationships over time.

## CHAPTER 11 ACTION PACKED DISCUSSION QUESTIONS

*1. What are your strongest relationships? What has made them last?*

*2. How can you show your gratitude to an adult who has helped guide you?*

*3. What are simple ways you can reach out to old connections?*

Chapter 12 Preface

# YOU CAN'T STAY FOREVER

In researching and connecting with young people for this book, I talked with a junior in high school from Delaware named Isabel. She is someone who has been very involved throughout high school doing things like Best Buddies, Science Olympiad, tennis, musicals, and ROTC.

She told me as a freshman in ROTC, the core-commander (a female upperclassman in her high school) pulled her aside and said, "Isabel, I know you're only a freshman, but I see a lot of potential in what you're doing."

This one moment gave Isabel a huge boost of confidence. She started to become a leader within her unit, but it didn't stop there.

Over time, Isabel's core-commander showed her exactly how to run the unit, and she didn't sugar-coat the things that needed to improve. She admitted to Isabel that there were times she could have done a better job. She was also honest with Isabel about struggles she had being in a leadership role.

The core-commander has since graduated high school, but the legacy she left has helped Isabel become a strong leader within the unit.

Isabel now looks to help other young people become strong leaders within the unit just as her core-commander did for her.

When talking to Isabel about her experience, she said something that really resonated with me, and I'd like to share it with you:

"You can't stay in high school forever. Your goal as a leader should be to hand off the torch and say, 'I've shown you what I could do now it's time for you to make it better.' Show people what you've done, train them, and be honest about your faults so that they can make it better."

This chapter is all about ensuring your hard work isn't forgotten when you move on to the next chapter in your life.

Building a legacy isn't easy and sometimes you won't even know about the legacy you've left for years down the road – maybe not at all.

I'm hoping this chapter will give you the perspective you need to do it effectively – and if nothing else, continue to help you *think* like leaders think about leaving the world better than you found it.

I'll talk about:

- The importance of leaving
- Your platform/what you stand for
- Holding others accountable
- Passing the torch

Chapter 12

# BUILDING A LEGACY

*"The legacy I would like to leave behind is a very simple one – that I have always stood up for what I consider to be the right thing, and I have tried to be as fair and equitable as I could be."*

—Ratan Tata

As a young leader, you will inevitably move on.

It may not feel like it at the moment, but you will eventually graduate, get a job, or go to college.[68]

Hopefully, your school and community will be just a little better off because you were a part of them. One of the best things you can do as a leader is to find ways to allow others to be successful and carry on whatever you were passionate about and worked hard on during your time in school.

This is your legacy.

---

[68] Or stay living at your parent's house without a job forever; I don't know what your life goals are.

Whatever your role as a leader, it's never too early or too late to start thinking about your legacy.

This chapter will discuss how to leave a positive and effective one.

## LEAVE

To leave a legacy, you have to do just that…leave.

Seems obvious, but it's more than just graduating and leaving old responsibilities behind. Seek out a new leader and pass the reigns along. Give them guidance, and you can ensure a piece of your leadership style is carried on in your absence.

It is the same reason why a book like this one must end. I have to stop writing so that you can start taking action. These lessons don't belong on paper. They belong alive in your thoughts and actions. My hope is to leave a legacy through these pages coming alive through *you* every day.

Former State Council Vice President of Tennessee 4-H, Caroline Brooks, told me:

"Being able to step back and know when it's time to hand off responsibilities to someone else or give someone else an opportunity is what makes a good leader. Allowing others to share their ideas, give their input, and be a part of the goal. A leader steps up and takes criticism when they need to, but also steps back to listen to their team when appropriate."

There always comes a time to let go of power and control, and trust your successors will step up to the plate.

## YOUR PLATFORM

In a literal sense, a platform is something you stand on.

Not so differently, a platform is usually used to describe the foundation for a thought or action.

Politicians use their platforms to put on display their non-negotiable values and goals. And while most of you will not run for political office, you still have a platform.

Your personal platform is the foundation of your character. Your platform is vital to your role as a leader and it sets a precedent for everything you do and say.

If, as a captain of a team, you have a zero-tolerance alcohol policy, enforcing that policy and living up to it yourself shows your strength as a leader. When it is your time to leave your role on the team, the captain coming after you will be tasked to fill your shoes as a strong leader and will already have the blueprint to do so.

Everything up until this point should have helped you define what your platform looks like – how your thoughts become your actions, and how intentionally defining your values will lead to a life of honesty and integrity.

Let your values guide you in making good decisions as a leader.

Establish a platform other leaders will aspire to emulate once you've moved on.

### YOU SAID IT!

*"Great leaders are people who can bring out the best qualities of the people around them. It's not about you."*

—BRADLEY REW
SOPHOMORE, RICHLAND HIGH SCHOOL

## HOLD OTHERS ACCOUNTABLE

Former NFL coach Bill Parcells once said, "You can't complain about what you don't enforce."

Don't be the person to complain about the government without acting on your opportunity to vote.

Don't complain about your grades if you haven't studied.

Don't expect the members of a group project to work hard if you aren't working hard.

Take action: hold yourself and others to the standards you hope to embody. Your *choices* as leader affect everyone, so make them good ones.

---

*In this generation we are constantly reminded of how cautious we, as young adults, must be when it comes to our behavior. Everything we do has the potential to be released to the world through posts, tweets, snaps, and various social media and this is also why building and maintaining a legacy is becoming more and more challenging. A good friend once told me to never do anything I wouldn't want broadcasted in Time Square, and now I am passing that advice to all of you. Being a student leader requires a great reputation because with that comes great respect and opportunities.*

—Riley Seaver
Former Washington DECA State Officer

---

## PASSING THE TORCH

It's great to be heavily involved, but sometimes you need to get out of the weeds.

This means stepping back, not having to personally deal with everything that comes up, and giving others ownership.

As you've already read, guiding others' work can lead to better outcomes than doing the work yourself. It allows others to be more invested and passionate, and instills within them the desire to see the group succeed.

Put a group in a position to operate without you, and it will continue to be successful once you pass the torch and move on.

• • •

When passing on a leadership role to the next leader, be sure to assist the new leader in the transition. Providing lists, written descriptions of responsibilities, or a calendar of events are all helpful, *tactical* things you can do if you are thinking about your legacy effectively.

Get creative. Find the best ways to give new leaders a blueprint for how to carry out tasks successfully.

As the group transitions without you, offer your assistance and advice from time to time, or just simply check in. Although the responsibility is no longer yours, part of building a legacy is doing what you can to ensure future success. Good luck!

## CHAPTER 12 ACTION PACKED DISCUSSION QUESTIONS

1. *What values make up your platform?*

2. *What do you want to see your organization accomplish after you've left?*

3. *How can you begin your legacy while you are still a leader?*

4. *What knowledge, skills, and abilities will the leader who takes your place need to be successful? How can you help prepare them?*

# EDDIE WOULD GO

The true value of leadership lies in our ability to take *action*.

Coming to understand our thoughts will help us do so.

All young people think – young leaders think differently.

Use the lessons throughout to direct your thinking, and allow your new thoughts to direct your actions.

*Your actions will define you.*

. . .

Eddie Aikau was a well-known Hawaiian lifeguard and surfer.

He is said to have saved over 500 people in his time on the North Shore of Oahu. Whenever someone needed help, Eddie was there.

At age 31, Eddie volunteered as a crewmember for a 30-day voyage on a double-hulled canoe. While on the voyage, the canoe sprung a leak during a storm and began to capsize.

In this moment, Eddie did what he had done so many times before – he sprang into action. He grabbed his surfboard from the canoe and began paddling into the storm in an attempt to get help.

Although the rest of the crew was later rescued by the U.S. Coast Guard, the search for Eddie does not have such a happy ending. Eddie was lost at sea and was never seen again.

While his final rescue attempt was unsuccessful, Eddie's legacy lives on to this day.

He is remembered for the years he spent pulling people out of waves no one else would dare to dive into.

He was confident in his abilities and bold enough to take action when others would not.

While I don't know exactly the thoughts going through Eddie's brain, I'd be willing to bet he made a conscious decision at some point in his life to put others before himself. I'd be willing to bet his actions in the scariest moments were simply a reflection of the way he *thought* at all times.

Today, t-shirts and bumper stickers can be seen around the world with the phrase, "Eddie Would Go."

People continue to be inspired by the legacy of Eddie Aikau and his lifetime of truly heroic action.

Student leaders must approach life with a similar philosophy to Eddie.

When opportunities arise, young leaders take action.

They build lives of *honesty* and *integrity* based in *positive thought*.

They courageously *care* for others even when it isn't the *cool* or "*safe*" thing to do.

They communicate, interact, and live their personal brand by filling their cup from the bottom with intentional characteristics – characteristics like *empathy*, *compassion*, and *generosity*.

Young leaders step up, just like Eddie, every day to build a legacy worth following.

If these things seem risky, consider the alternative – never doing anything of purpose, putting people down, and floating through life without any sort of vision or direction.

I would argue becoming a young leader and following the fearless legacy of Eddie is actually less of a risk – it is your true chance to find *purpose* in your life. To find meaning and feel the fulfillment that comes with using every day to get one step closer to who you'd like to *become* – this is what thinking like a leader is all about.

It shouldn't be a secret anymore: *Anyone can lead.*

You picked up this book – you have the *desire*.

And you've made it this far – you have the *knowledge*.

You've got everything you need to be a leader in high school.

With knowledge and desire comes the responsibility to *make something happen*.

I personally challenge you to put your positive thoughts into *action*.

Take the leap into leadership.

Go for it.

If you succeed, congratulations. If you fail, dust yourself off, learn from your mistakes, and try again. That's what *Action Packed Leadership* is all about.

Take all the lessons in this book with you, and like Eddie, be *daring* in your attempts to make the world a better place.

**Young leaders shape the future of our world and you are one of them.**

What will you do with your power? Where will you go? Will you go boldly in the direction of becoming the best version of yourself?

Eddie would go.

Will you?

# ACKNOWLEDGMENTS

A huge thank you to my wife, Danielle, for being so patient and loving with my busy schedule and ambitious dreams. You're wonderful.

To my ever-growing family, thank you for being there for me in my business and personal life. Thank you for supporting me and bringing so much joy into my life. I love you all - Monte, Patti, John, Allison, Avery, Bryan, Anna, Vincent, Fiona, Walter, Erin, Josh, Madison, and Emma.

To my "Speaker Friends" who have encouraged my growth through the years so I can better reach the youth I intend to serve. You all mean more to me than you know - I admire you and appreciate your work. Specifically, Jake Kelfer, Brandon White, Shannon McKain, Scott Backovich, Kate Garnes, Phil Boyte, Micah Jacobson, Houston Kraft, John Norlin, Esteban Gast, Harriett Turk, Isaac Butts, Dr. Laymon Hicks, Heather Schultz, and Geoff McLachlan.

To the leadership and members of the organization I grew up in and still work with today - Wisconsin DECA – especially Tim Fandek (and Bennett Fandek for some great title suggestions), Terri Mackey, Keegan O'Brien, Jackie Page, and all the State Officers I've had the pleasure of working with (from Team 47 until now) – thank you for giving me feedback and allowing me the opportunity to continue building meaningful leadership content over the years.

To all the people who contributed in some way to making this book what it is – from the early days of researching leadership topics to the finished product. Thank you to Niel Patel for your extensive effort to bring this book to the finish line – and Shyam Patel for being the first middle school student to read the book and give feedback. Thank you to Mila Milic for your wonderful design abilities and James Saleska for your formatting and design skills. Thank you to Hannah Trudeau, Sara Nilles, Eli Holm, Bill Martin, Dr. Michelle McGrath, Dalton

Green, Cathleen Taylor, and Ashley Tessmer for giving me such expert feedback and advice.

Thank you to the "Student Experts" who contributed their expertise to this book and other Action Packed Leadership programs – some of these exceptional students are highlighted throughout this book. A specific thank you goes out to Kayla Spencer, Jaron May, Christina Wenman, Isaiah Swift, and Rachel Brosman for your exceptional examples of what student leadership looks like in action.

Thank you to Chris Fisher for continuing to support my work as a speaker and the work you do to help young people in so many ways.

Thank you to Mitch McMahon and Madeline Guyette for supporting Action Packed Leadership from the very beginning.

A big shout-out to all the teachers, advisors, administrators, and coaches who work with young people day-in and day-out to help build up the next generation of leaders. Thank you for all the work you do – especially for the meaningful moments you create with students that so often go unnoticed.

Last but certainly not least, thank you, God, for everything You do in my life.

# ABOUT THE AUTHOR

Kyle Willkom is a sought-after keynote speaker, workshop facilitator, and educational consultant. He is the founder of Action Packed Leadership, LLC – a leadership development company focused on helping young people become the best versions of themselves.

Kyle's two previous books on leadership have been read around the world and used in leadership programs to facilitate meaningful discussions. Wake Up Call is the story of a high school student who, after experiencing an unexpected loss, encounters 5 unforgettable people who help him cope and move forward in a healthy and positive way. Kyle often refers to his second book, The Thinking Dilemma, as the Snapchat of leadership books; it is quick-hitting and easy to read. The book moves fast and encourages readers to think intentionally about maximizing their short-term and long-term happiness.

Through Kyle's speaking, books, and online resources, he has reached hundreds of thousands of young people with messages of kindness, positivity, and action.

In his free time, Kyle enjoys going on outdoor adventures with his wife, Danielle, eating pizza, and watching Milwaukee Bucks basketball games.

To learn more about Kyle or to book him to speak, visit www.kylewillkom.com.

# INTERVIEWS

A special thank you to the exceptional young leaders below for taking the time to chat with me about their stories and, ultimately, what leadership looks like in high school.

Alyssa Comins
Becky Carlson
Bradley Rew
Caroline Brooks
Carter Cleaves
Dalton Green
Dana Ahmed
Grace Franz
Hannah Swedberg
Jaspreet Singh
Katie Brown
Kayla Spencer
Lexi Franklin
Lynn Tomlinson
McKayla Gilbert
Mike Seely
Morgan Rajala
Nick Yochum
Niel Patel
Rachel Wagner
Riley Seaver
Will Dalton

I wish I could include the names of the countless students and teachers I've spoken to informally at conferences and schools around the country – the list above is nowhere near complete. If we've spent time together chatting about leadership, know that you hold a special place in my heart.

# NOTES

***Chapter 1: Business Communication***

Horn, Sam. "What is the Eyebrow Test?" *The Intrigue Agency*. The Intrigue Agency, 3 Feb. 2012. Web. 7 June 2014. <http://samhornpop.wordpress.com/>.

Lenhart, Amanda, Rich Ling, Scott Campbell, and Kristen Purcell. "Teens and Mobile Phones." *Pew Research Center: Internet, Science, and Tech*. Pew Research Center, 20 April 2012. Web. 16 June 2014. <http://www.pewinternet.org/2010/04/20/teens-and-mobile-phones/>.

Mehrabian, Albert. *Nonverbal Communication*. Chicago: Aldine-Atherton, 1972. Print.

"Presumptuous." *Merriam-Webster*. Merriam-Webster, n.d. Web. 16 July 2014. <http://www.merriam-webster.com/dictionary/presumptuous>.

Uebelherr, Jan. "Father John Naus, Beloved Marquette Professor for Half a Century, Dies." *Milwaukee Wisconsin Journal Sentinel*. Journal Sentinel, Inc., 23 Sept. 2013. Web. 10 September 2014. < http://www.jsonline.com/news/obituaries/father-john-naus-beloved-marquette-professor-for-half-decade-dies-b99104242z1-224851922.html>.

***Chapter 2: Personal Branding***

Goman, Carol K. "Seven Seconds to make a First Impression." Forbes. Forbes Magazine, 13 Feb. 2011. Web. 16 June 2014. <http://www.forbes.com/sites/carolkinseygoman/2011/02/13/seven-seconds-to-make-a-first-impression/>.

Krueger, Alyson. "12 Statistic-Driven Ways to Make Lasting First Impressions." Business Insider. Business Insider, Inc., 16 Dec. 2010. Web. 16 June 2015. <http://www.businessinsider.com/20-ways-to-nail-a-good-first-impression-2010-12?op=1>.

Llopis, Glenn. "Personal Branding Is A Leadership Requirement, Not a Self-Promotion Campaign." Forbes. Forbes Magazine, 8 April 2013. Web. 2 July 2014. <http://www.forbes.com/sites/glennllopis/2013/04/08/personal-branding-is-a-leadership-requirement-not-a-self-promotion-campaign/>.

## Chapter 3: Taking Initiative

"Mark Zuckerberg's letter to investors: 'The Hacker Way.'" CNN Money. Cable News Network, 1 Feb. 2012. Web. 16 June 2015. <http://money.cnn.com/2012/02/01/technology/zuckerberg_ipo_letter/>.

## Chapter 4: Project Management

"Study Focuses on Strategies for Achieving Goals, Resolutions." Dominican University of California. Dominican University of Califiornia, n.d. Web. 3 July 2014. <http://www.dominican.edu/dominicannews/study-backs-up-strategies-for-achieving-goals>.

## Chapter 5: Networking

"6 Tips for a Good Handshake." Etiquette International. Etiquette International, n.d. Web. 17 June 2014. <http://www.etiquetteinternational.com/Tips/handshake.aspx>.

Marr, Bernard. "If You Want to Impress a Stranger, Here Are the Body Language Mistakes to Avoid." Quartz. Quartz, 9 July 2014. Web. 14 July 2014. <http://qz.com/231866/here-are-the-body-language-mistakes-you-should-avoid-making-with-strangers/>.

"Networking." BusinessDictionary.com. WebFinance,Inc, n.d. Web. 11 July 2014. <http://www.businessdictionary.com/definition/networking.html>.

"Networking." Yale Office of Career Strategy. Yale University, 2014. Web. 11 July 2014. <http://ucs.yalecollege.yale.edu/content/networking>.

Pappas, Stephanie. "First Impressions Hard to Change, Studies Suggest." LiveScience. TechMedia Network, 18 Feb. 2014. Web. 14 July 2014. <http://www.livescience.com/43439-first-impressions-hard-to-change.html>.

Quast, Lisa. "5 Tips for Creating a Positive First Impression." *Forbes*. Forbes Magazine, 9 Sept. 2013. Web. 11 July 2014. <http://www.forbes.com/sites/lisaquast/2013/09/09/5-tips-to-create-a-positive-first-impression/>.

Shin, Laura. "How to Use LinkedIn: 5 Smart Steps to Career Success." Forbes. Forbes Magazine, 26 July 2014. Web. 16 June 2014. <http://www.forbes.com/sites/laurashin/2014/06/26/how-to-use-linkedin-5-smart-steps-to-career-success/ >.

Smith, Jacquelyn. "How Much Coworker Socializing is Good for Your Career?" Forbes. Forbes Magazine, 24 Sept. 2013. Web. 11 July 2014. http://www.forbes.com/sites/jacquelynsmith/2013/09/24/how-much-coworker-socializing-is-good-for-your-career/

Vaynerchuck, Gary. "You're Focusing on the Wrong Stuff." Medium. Gary Vaynerchuk, 28 May 2014 Web. 7 July 2014. < https://medium.com/@garyvee/youre-focusing-on-the-wrong-stuff-543aed6168e5>.

*Chapter 6: Time Management*

Matthews, Joe, Don Debolt and Deb Percival. "10 Time Management Tips that Work." Entrepreneur. Entrepreneur Media, Inc., n.d. Web. 16 July 2014. <http://www.entrepreneur.com/article/219553>.

McKay, Brett and Kate McKay. "The Eisenhower Decision Matrix: How to Distinguish Between Urgent and Important Tasks and Make Real Progress in Your Life." The Art of Manliness. The Art of Manliness, 23 Oct. 2013. Web. 16 July 2014. <http://www.artofmanliness.com/2013/10/23/eisenhower-decision-matrix/>.

Pattison, Kermit. "Worker, Interrupted: The Cost of Task Switching." Fast Company. Fast Company & Inc., 28 July 2008. Web. 17 July 2014. http://www.fastcompany.com/944128/worker-interrupted-cost-task-switching.

Yates, Diana. "Brief Diversions Vastly Improve Focus, Researchers Find." News Bureau: Illinois. News Bureau: Public Affairs University of Illinois, 8 Feb. 2011. Web. 18 July 2014. <http://www.news.illinois.edu/news/11/0208focus_AlejandroLleras.html>.

## NOTES

*Chapter 7: Working Smarter*

Covey, Stephen. The 7 Habits of Highly Effective People. New York: Free Press. 1989. Print.

*Chapter 9: Building Trust*

Horsager, David. "You Can't Be a Great Leader Without Trust. Here's How You Build It." Forbes. Forbes Magazine, 24 Oct. 2012. Web. 22 July 2014. <http://www.forbes.com/sites/forbesleadershipforum/2012/10/24/you-cant-be-a-great-leader-without-trust-heres-how-you-build-it/>.

"Persian carpet." Wikipedia. Wikipedia, n.d. Web. 1 July 2015. http://en.wikipedia.org/wiki/Persian_carpet

*Chapter 10: Staying Motivated*

Parker, Sam. "212 Degrees: The Extra Degree." Online video clip. YouTube. YouTube, 13 June 2013. Web. 11 August 2014. <https://www.youtube.com/watch?v=e82_Z6-tGaY>.

*Chapter 11: Maintaining Relationships*

"Altruism." Merriam-Webster. Merriam-Webster, n.d. Web. 16 July 2014, <http://www.merriam-webster.com/thesaurus/altruistic>.

Kreitzer, Mary Joe. "Why Personal Relationships are Important." University of Minnesota. Regents of the University of Minnesota and Charlson Meadows, n.d. Web. 11 August, 2014. <http://www.takingcharge.csh.umn.edu/enhance-your-wellbeing/relationships/why-personal-relationships-are-important>.

*Chapter 12: Building a Legacy*

Ferrazzi, Keith. *Never Eat Alone*. New York City: Doubleday, 2005. Print.

*Conclusion*

"Eddie Aiku." *Wikipedia: The Free Encyclopedia*. Wikimedia Foundation, Inc, n.d. Web. 9 Sept. 2014 <http://en.wikipedia.org/wiki/Eddie_Aikau>.

Made in the USA
Monee, IL
31 July 2020